Wives of Catholic Clergy

Joseph H. Fichter

Sheed & Ward

Sheed & Ward™ is a service of National Catholic Reporter Publishing Company, Inc.

Library of Congress Cataloguing-in-Publication Data

·Fichter, Joseph Henry, 1908-
    Wives of Catholic clergy / Joseph H. Fichter.
      p.   cm.
    Includes bibliographical references and index.
    ISBN 1-55612-474-0 (alk. paper)
    1. Clergymen's wives. 2. Catholic Church—Clergy. 3. Women in the Catholic Church. I. Title.
    BV4395.F49   1992
    282'.082—dc20   91-45845
                                                CIP

Published by: Sheed & Ward
                 115 E. Armour Blvd. P.O. Box 419492
                 Kansas City, MO 64141-6492

To order, call: (800) 333-7373

Cover design by John Murello.

Contents

Introduction

One of the less admirable characteristics of historical Catholicism has been its record of sexism and clericalism, a pattern of discrimination that has kept Catholic women "in their place" over the centuries. This systematic tradition of gender inequality has become the object of frequent attack by feminists. When the American Bishops first proposed to write a pastoral letter on the subject of women in the Church, they were advised by feminists not to do so. The problem, they argued, is not the women but the patriarchy. The most radical feminist demand is that there cannot be equality between the sexes in the Catholic Church until the patriarchal structure is dismantled.

The focus of this book is not on the problem of male dominance, but on the women who have survived within a patriarchal system that seems so permanent. The Catholic hierarchy looked with disfavor on the American Movement for Women's Rights, initiated at Seneca Falls in 1848. Women's suffrage was an evil because it would lead Catholic women to listen to the politicians rather than the clergy. They would no longer be obedient to their husbands. Cardinal Gibbons once declared that "the women's rights movement was the worst enemy of the female sex."

Too much schooling was not good for Catholic girls. It made them discontented and unfit for Catholic womanhood. The bishops opposed Child Labor Laws because they interfered with the authority of parents over their children. In the long and unsuccessful struggle for the Equal Rights Amendment, a few leaders, like Father Hesburgh and Bishop Hunthausen, were supportive, but the National Council of Catholic Women actually voted against the ERA.

Organized religion is seldom in the forefront of significant social movements, and change for the better in the women's liberation movement has been slower in the Roman Church than in other Christian denominations. A kind of ecclesiastical "breakthrough" occurred at Philadelphia in 1974 when three retired bishops "irregularly" ordained eleven women to the Episcopal priesthood. American Catholics experienced their own sudden "breakthrough" six years later, with the Vatican decision, "Pastoral Provisions," which allowed some priests to have wives.

The fact that the National Conference of Catholic Bishops petitioned the Holy See for the right to ordain married men came as a surprise to American Catholics. The Vatican listed these provisions as the guide for the introduction of married convert Episcopal clergy to the Roman Catholic priesthood. It is an ecclesiastical experiment which indirectly approves women in the role of clergy wives. The book-length study I published in 1989, about this unusual phenomenon, is a logical preliminary to a further investigation of the status of women in the Catholic tradition. My sociological interest in women's liberation is an extension of the research I have conducted about priests and parishes and Catholic institutions over several decades. In all our studies we have seen that women are the "best" Catholics, representing Christian ideals in belief and behavior at a higher level than males. Their religious way of life was ideologically essential to institutional Catholicism, but it has always been functionally subordinate to males and clergy.

To go back to the beginning, the Catholic women about whom we know the least historically are the wives of the clergy, starting with the Apostles, bishops, presbyters, and deacons of early Christianity. Even though prelates and priests continued for more than a thousand years to marry and to father children, we know little or nothing about their wives, whose life experiences, and even their names, have been erased. The only generalizations we can reasonably propose is that they participated in the Christian faith, were sacramentally married, produced children, took care of husband, home and family.

Although we have no historical details about the personal biography of this multitude of Catholic wives and mothers who lived and worked with their clergy husbands, we have to surmise that they led exemplary lives in the midst of the Christian community. The Levitical tradition was a marrying tradition, and the development of the Christian priesthood included the presence of the wife and children. The seeds of celibacy and enkratism were there from the very beginning, but they took many centuries to blossom sufficiently to interfere effectively with the married priesthood.

The pattern of clergy marriage was not seriously threatened during the first millennium of the Christian Church, but the so-called "Fathers" of the Church, like Jerome, Cyril, and Peter Damian, carried on a consistent barrage of opposition against the mothers who bore children to clergy husbands. A peculiar thesis on sexuality evolved to the point where marital relations of the clergy were suspect as the temptation of the devil. Women were the sexual source of the devil's work in the world, even in sacramental marriage. Consistent efforts of the Church hierarchy to forbid the marriage of clerics reached a climax in the prohibitions of the Council of Trent. The Latin Church then placed an absolute ban against the marriage of priests.

Despite the eventual denigration of clergy wives, the Christian ministry was largely sustained through the centuries by the zealous activities of women. The earliest recognition is given to the widows who worked individually and collectively in support of their needy fellow Christians. The widows became an ecclesial order, or primitive congregation, who led virtuous lives while carrying out the corporal works of mercy. In accord with the contemporary culture they were willing to forego a second marriage on the death of their husband. This was a free and voluntary decision and not bound by public vows. They were ministering to the needy in the midst of the world, not withdrawn and secluded.

Another category of devout and dedicated women was in the order of virgins, which evolved as a recognized status for women who did not want to marry. To remain celibate for the sake of the Gospel was a personal decision that was probably infrequent in the first two centuries after the death of Christ. Gradually, however, virginity became institutionalized under the guidance of the hierarchy. As the numbers of virgins increased, they began to gather in religious congregations and were, for the most part, loosely organized. They were not set apart as a separate ministry in the Church and were not committed to any specific personal or social role. Theirs was the exemplary life of prayer and devotion.

The third type of ecclesial women in early Christianity was the order of deaconesses, who emerged in the third century as an important contribution to church ministry. There appears to have been an incipient system of gender segregation in ministry; deacons ministered to males, deaconesses to females. It appears also that deaconesses, unlike deacons, were deprived of the sacrament of holy orders. Indeed, they gradually disappeared, or were absorbed, into the cloistered and monastic congregations about the fifth century. The cloister then became the way of life for women who dedicated themselves to the service of God.

The religious vocation for Catholic women, their ministry in the Church of Christ, was characterized by the evangelical counsels of poverty, chastity and obedience. Parallel congregations for women were established by the Benedictines, Carmelites, Franciscans, and Dominicans. The popular notion, for a long time encouraged by spiritual writers and church authorities, was that the religious vocation was a higher status than the vocation to marriage. The congregations of contemplative nuns were soon outnumbered by the "active" orders whose members expanded the Christian ministry of education, health care, social welfare, and foreign missions.

The growth of the American Sisterhoods was spectacular, until the peak was reached of about 180,000 nuns at the time of the Second Vatican Council. Although the numbers have drastically declined, the ministerial activities of the Sisters expanded enormously within the Church. They conduct retreats for the laity, assume chaplaincies in hospitals and universities, and take over the administration of priestless parishes. It is not unusual now to find Sisters at work in chancery offices, as presidents of diocesan school boards, directors of Catholic charities, and other diocesan committees. They are gradually approaching equal occupational status with the clergy, an historical advance from their traditional position of subservience in the Church structure.

The discussion of Catholic women, organized over the centuries in various forms of institutionalized ministry, must not take attention away from the great majority of lay women who faithfully professed the Christian religion. Although the authority and administration of the Roman Church has always been in the hands of males, the common practice of the faith has always been predominantly feminine. The fact that females are more religious than males has been consistently recognized throughout Christian history, even though no satisfactory explanation, psychological or sociological, has been forthcoming from research. This is not simply a matter of personal spirituality, the religious relationship with God. It is the women who vitalize the parochial and diocesan programs of the Church, who perform the everyday tasks of the Christian ministry.

The Catholic hierarchy has been slow to recognize and support women's liberation in the larger society, where the right to vote and to receive just wages has been affirmed. In the institutional church, the feminist movement for equal rights was picked up first by the religious Sisters. Networks of mutual support were established of Sisters congregations to represent their own push for progress. One of the more vocal movements in the Church is the Women's Ordination Conference, promoted over the years by St. Joan's Alliance. The numbers of Catholic women who aspire to the priesthood are still relatively few, but their demands are as persistent as they are futile. There are many areas of church activity, other than the ordained priesthood, in which women may minister.

The prospect of women becoming the spouses of the clergy depends upon whether the Church grants approval for married clergy. Women were in the forefront of the organization of the National Association for Pastoral Renewal. Neither the Vatican nor the American hierarchy took seriously this request for a married priesthood, under the title of "Optional Celibacy." The request for a change in the rules continues unabated with the reorganization of CORPUS, now known as the National Association for a Married Priesthood. The Fathers of the Second Vatican Council were forbidden to discuss the law of celibacy, and the Vatican officialdom has consistently prevented it from becoming a topic of discussion at the Bishops' Synods. Thousands of priests have petitioned the Holy See for permission to marry, even while continuing in the active ministry.

Even when a rescript is granted to allow marriage, there is a simultaneous "reduction" of the priest to the status of the laity. The fact is that the great majority of these priests do not want to quit the ministry; they have not "lost" their vocation, but they want to continue in the ministry with a wife at their side. More and more of the resigned priests are unwilling to accept the notion that marriage is incompatible with priesthood. They do not admit that they were "unsuitable" candidates for ordination to the priesthood, or that they had failed as priests. They insist that "once a priest always a priest," and are unwilling to call themselves "ex-priests" or "former priests." They want to remain in the priesthood while also taking the option to marry.

The traditional preliminary approach to the priesthood has been the so-called minor order of the diaconate. Every aspirant to the priesthood is first a transitional deacon, which means that he takes this preliminary step toward the celibate priesthood. The "revival" of the married diaconate, which apparently flourished in the Apostolic Age, has made a ministerial opening for married men and their wives. We were able to obtain personal information from these wives who are quite enthusiastic about the ministry of their husbands. In general, they do not see this experience as a step to the priesthood for their husbands, nor do they express a desire for women's ordination, either to the diaconate or the priesthood.

What was unique about the Pastoral Provisions for the acceptance of Episcopal-priest converts was not the fact of their turning to Rome. That happens all the time, just as there is a steady march of Roman priests annually converting to the Episcopal Church, where the normal priestly ministry is shared with wives. What is unique about the document of "provisions" is that they were allowed to bring their wives with them while they continued in the active ministry. I searched out these "new" wives—who are not numerous—to find out how they approached this unique role of priest-wife.

For the most part, these wives were friendly and cooperative in interviews and questionnaires, even though their official "coordinator," Father Luther Parker, advised them not to talk about themselves. The reason for secrecy is not clear, although Father Parker said that "the Catholic authorities asked for confidentiality" about this whole procedure. The bishops may have wanted to play down these conversions for the sake of ecumenical goodwill with the Episcopalians. Perhaps they wanted also to "tone down" the shock of introducing priests' wives into the rigidly celibate climate of American Catholicism.

The statistics of our enquiry among the wives of convert priests suggest that the procedures for their transfer to the Catholic Church were often cumbersome and dilatory. Nevertheless, once they have settled down to the Catholic marital and familial routine, they express themselves quite satisfied and even enthusiastic. The personal story of one of the wives, Mary Dally, describes the whole procedure as a narrative of delays and tribulations, of joys and achievements. Her autobiographical *Married to a Catholic Priest* is personal and unique, but it serves as a paradigm of the manner in which the wife of an Episcopal priest makes a "Journey of Faith" to become the wife of a Roman Catholic priest.

In contrast to this small number of "new" clergy wives, there are large numbers of other wives who believe that they and their husbands should be welcomed into the ranks of the Catholic priesthood. Thousands of "defrocked" priests who are now married are willing to return to the active ministry, together with their wives. These wives differ from the convert wives because their husbands have been "reduced" to the status of laity. Since ordination is a permanent vocation, these women rightly claim marriage to a priest, even while their husbands are not permitted to function in the active ministry.

The ecclesial status of these wives, like that of their husbands, is completely and officially non-clerical. They are not recognized by either prelates, or people, as the wives of Catholic clergy. Yet, they are not likely to fade into oblivion, because they are actively engaged in the program of the National Association for a Married Priesthood. At the same time, they continue to practice as parishioners, bring up their children in the faith, and do the volunteer church activities characteristic of Catholic female parishioners.

Women who are romantically involved with priests outside the marital relationship are sometimes blamed for seducing the celibate clergy. Perhaps more often, they are seen as victims of sexually deviant priests. Stories of unchaste priests who take advantage of women, and leave them abandoned, appear frequently in the *National Catholic Reporter* and in the public press. These love relationships range from the relatively innocent "third way" to long settled domiciles where the wife and children reside, while the priest continues to perform undetected in the active ministry. In between these two polar examples are the women who are sexually active—carrying on an affair—with clergy who are reluctant to leave the priesthood for marriage.

The law of celibacy is essentially a law of sexual abstinence, but it does not exclude a celibate relationship of Platonic love, or Christian *caritas*. This is the common and virtuous experience of Christian love between the sexes, in which sexual desire has been suppressed or sublimated. The point at which platonic love begins to evolve into romantic love is the point at which the priest must decide whether or not to resign the priesthood. When he drifts into a sexual relationship, with no intention or prospect of marriage, he is said to be "having an affair" which may become a public scandal.

In these illicit relationships between a woman and a priest, the common male chauvinist attitude is that it is the woman who is "at fault." The male tendency is to demean the woman who is subject to this humiliation, and it is the woman who "pays" for the transgression while the priest continues to operate under the cloak of presumed chastity.

The marriages of resigned priests, which began after the Second Vatican Council, have multiplied and endured to the extent that they have produced a new generation of "preachers' kids." In our study of their attitudes, the young adult offspring (15 years and older) do not suggest that their father was a failure as a priest, or that their mother made a mistake in marrying a priest. We have responses from 233 of these youngsters, whose parents are members of the National Association for a Married Priesthood. More than half (55%) were the children of resigned nuns. They recognize that their fathers are "older" than the fathers of friends. They feel that early life in the seminary, or convent, cheated their parents from having a normal adolescence, so that they do not understand teenagers.

Half of them attended neither elementary or secondary Catholic schools, and about half are not involved in their parish. Yet, they attend Mass and receive Holy Communion more frequently than other young Catholics. But they do not escape the trend to secularism so common among American youths. The youngest category (15-16 years old) rates higher in beliefs and behavior than the oldest category (19 years and older). One of the noteworthy facts is that 28 percent express an interest in following a church vocation.

As may be expected, they are overwhelmingly in favor of the married priesthood, and the majority think that the Church should admit women to the priesthood. They tend to be "liberal" also in their attitudes on social issues. They oppose capital punishment and reductions in social welfare programs. They are in support of alien immigrants who have come in illegally.

If the lower clergy in the Roman Church were given the option to marry or to remain celibate, should not the same option be open to the episcopate? The answer given by two out of five (38%) priests in an earlier survey was that bishops ought to marry. More recently, Terrence Sweeney found that one out of four (24%) bishops agreed that priests be allowed to marry, but ventured no opinion about the marriage of bishops. At the present time, and under the urging of Pope John Paul, the American Bishops are constrained to promote clerical celibacy. They are saddened by the exodus of so many of their priests—friends and former classmates—who opt for marriage. There is no reason to suggest that the bishops do not feel the same stress—loneliness, frustration, that brings dissatisfaction with celibacy to the lower clergy.

Aside from the proscriptions of the Vatican, one may suggest sociological advantages in a married episcopacy. As husbands and fathers of families, they would be much closer to the human condition experienced by the majority of adult Catholics. We permit ourselves to think that a married hierarchy could better understand a married clergy, as well as the family life of the laity. Not the least benefit would have to be an enormously improved relationship with Catholic womanhood, and a benevolent acceptance of the wives of the clergy.

Chapter One

Historical Clergy Wives

Jesus was born into the traditional Jewish society, which paid high respect to family life, to marriage and children, and perhaps especially to the families of the Levitical priesthood. The numerous ancestors of Jesus, as listed in the beginning of Matthew's gospel, had to include the names of some priests. In his humanity then, Jesus was most likely the descendent of a priestly lineage. The mother of John the Baptist was the spouse of a priest, named Zacharia, "who belonged to the priestly order of Abiah." Indeed, he was serving at the altar when the Angel of the Lord told him that his elderly wife was to bear a son. (Luke 1:8-14) Nothing is known of Anna and Joachim, the parents of Mary, but one is allowed to speculate piously that her father may also have been a priest.[1]

Jesus grew up in a community where friends and neighbors experienced normal family life and where marriage was the normal vocation of Jewish youth. His contemporary, Rabbi Hillel, said that the Hebrew family should have a minimum of two children, one boy and one girl. The people who gathered to hear Jesus preach were just normal citizens of the area, living out a daily pattern in their homes and neighborhoods. In other words, they were parents and children, among them priests, who were deeply impressed with the words of Jesus, his teachings and healings. They became the disciples of Christ and were the members of the new Christian community.

Very little has been recorded about the wives of priests, either of the Old Testament or of the early Christian community.[2] The earliest Christian clergy had to be the Apostles, or elders, who were recognized as bishops and deacons in the letters of St. Paul. Except for those who made missionary journeys, these early followers of Christ lived at home with their families, in their households, tended by the wife and mother. With the probable exception of John, the Apostles are all presumed to have been married men. Scripture experts now agree that the majority of clergy in the early Church were married men. The evangelist Philip had "four unmarried daughters who preached God's word." (Acts 21:9) The New Testament writings are generally silent about the home life of early Christians, especially about the wives of priests and their children.

Thousands of Jewish converts to Christ, who lived in Jerusalem and its environs, continued to go to the Temple, offered the sacrifices, observed the Mosaic law, but gathered on Sundays in their numerous households where the Eucharist was celebrated by the father of the family. They were already repeating the "Last Supper" of Christ and His apostles, and recalled its similarity with the Jewish Passover meal, which had also been an annual domestic ritual. Aside from the Eucharist and other private devotions, which sometimes attracted relatives and friends, the home was also the place of assembly of Christians in the vicinity. According to Acts 12:12, they often gathered and prayed at the home of Mark's mother in Jerusalem.

Early House Churches

Who but the wife and mother of the family maintained the home that came to be known as a "house church?" Harrington says that Jesus "showed little or no interest in establishing a highly structured organization or a new religion."[3] It was in the family setting where Christ's teachings took hold. Separate church buildings for Christian public worship were far in the future. In reference to the family, Meeks remarks that "the local structure of the early Christian groups was thus linked with what was commonly regarded as the basic unit of the society."[4]

It was also outside of Rome that the whole Christian movement found its pastoral basis in the family house. They met at the house of Philemon in Colossae (Phil. 2); in the house of

Nympha in Laodicea (Col. 4:15); in the home of Aquila and Priscilla in Ephesus (I Cor. 16:19). Schillebeeckx points out that the beginning of Christianity was in the "household of the faith." (Gal. 6:10) "The house was the place where there was preaching or instruction, and also the place where people ate and drank together, celebrated the Eucharist, and so on."[5]

Even without abundant evidence we may surmise that the religious assembly and the Eucharistic meal were presided over by the head of the household, who was a married man with a family. "This connection between family life and church life was so close that people expected their church officials to have the same qualities as a good head of a family, who, in union with his wife knew how to keep his household in good order." These church leaders were always males, mature, married men, who had the qualities of good "ministers" to the family and to the faith community. Schillebeeckx adds, "there is no indication of any rejection of women or of sexuality in connection with the priesthood."[6]

In the three decades after the death of Christ, and before the destruction of the Temple (70 A.D.), the Christians were not reluctant to "go up to the temple to pray," and to visit the synagogue on the Sabbath. There was not a complete breakaway from the Jewish past but a gradual drift toward the new and different liturgy. "Thus, it was, in fact, in the setting of private homes that the service of the word, in all its forms, originally found its most acceptable, most frequent and certainly its most favorable base. In particular, as was natural, the endless advantages that a home had to offer, as regards hospitality, social relationships and human contacts, seem to have been spontaneously recognized from the first, both by those who offered and by those who received hospitality."[7]

Missionary Wives

One of the few facts we know about the wives of the Apostles is that they accompanied their husbands on missionary trips and on visits to the increasing number of Christian congregations. Paul himself did not have a wife, but he said the other apostles certainly had a right to do this. We do not know whether the wives preached the Gospel, acted as secretary for their husbands, ministered to the women of the congregation, or were there mainly to care for their husbands. (I Cor. 9:5)

Perhaps the best-known reference to Peter's marital status is the account of Jesus healing the fever of his mother-in-law. "Jesus went to Peter's home, and there he saw Peter's mother-in-law sick in bed with a fever. He touched her hand, the fever left her, and she got up and began to wait on him." (Mt. 8:14-15) In his first letter to Timothy, Paul took it for granted that the Church leaders, whom he would now call priests and bishops, were married men with children. It may seem odd to us that Paul says he "must have only one wife," as though there were the likelihood of polygamy. The elder has to be a gentle person who knows how to manage his family. If he cannot do this, "how can he take care of the Church of God?" (I Tim 3:15) He gave exactly the same advice to Church "helpers" who were most likely the appointed deacons and part of the married clergy of the young Church.

Paul seems to be saying that domestic and fatherly qualities are most helpful in the direction of the growing congregations. As Brown remarks, "Since the Church is the 'household of God' (I Tim 3:15), a comparison heightened because the church met in a house, the presbyter-bishops are to be like fathers taking responsibility for a home, administering its goods and providing example and discipline. Stability and close relationship similar to that of a family home will hold the church together against the disintegrating forces that surround it or invade it."[8] It seems most obvious that the wife and mother is at the center of the stable Christian family.

Neither in ancient Judaism nor in early Christianity did the woman serve at the altar. The Jewish mother played a significant role in the family, which did not transfer to a significant role in institutionalized Judaism. The religion of the Jew has always been patriarchal and male-dominated. There were no Jewish priestesses, nor were the women ever engaged in priestly tasks. The early Christians tended to follow the culture patterns of contemporary Jewish society. While the Christian women logically prepared the Eucharistic meal for the family and community, and devoutly participated with the others, there is no record of her ever "celebrating" the sacrament.

When the Christian community settled in the Roman society, they were faced with a different pattern of female religious participation. Roman society allowed and encouraged women to assume religious leadership. We are told that "women played an essential part in the celebration of Roman religion. The wife shared responsibility with her husband for supervising the household cult. Apart from the Vestal Virgins, whose function was official and important, the wives of two of the major priests were themselves priestesses. Women had cults and ceremonies from which men were excluded (and vice versa). The Christian practice of keeping women away from the altar was to be a departure from Roman custom."[9]

Status of Christian Wives

Whatever the status of women in the Jewish tradition, one may imagine that the wife of a deacon, priest or bishop in apostolic times was held in some regard. Then, the spread of Christianity and the passage of time extended widely the pattern of married clergy. Among the Eastern Orthodox "there was no discrimination against married bishops and no distinction between married and unmarried candidates for the episcopate." Constantelos points out that "there were many married bishops in the early and medieval Eastern Church. Gregory of Nyssa, Gregory the Elder of Nazianzus, Kyros of Kotyaion, Gregory the Illuminator, as well as his successors to the Catholicate of Armenia, were married bishops."[10] In spite of the prohibitions laid down by the Council of Elvira, "married bishops attended the Synod of Rimini as well as other councils. Thus, in both the East and the West, the Church was flexible and there were married clergymen in all ranks."

In the middle of the third century, Cyprian was instructed and baptized a Christian by a saintly married priest, Caecilius, with whom he had a lasting friendship. At the point of death Caecilius asked Bishop Cyprian to be the "guardian of his wife and children."[11] The earliest attempt to place restrictions on the marital relations of the clergy was made at the Council of Elvira, with the decree that priests were to "abstain completely from their wives, and not to have children." Elvira acknowledged the fact of clerical marriage and did not decree divorce or that the wives be evicted from the home. Husband and wife could remain married but they were to change their "carnal union into a spiritual marriage." This decree did not break up marriage and family, and did not relieve the parents from maintaining and supporting their household.

The prohibition of Elvira, if it had any real effect, was probably heeded only in the South of Spain. Elsewhere among the multiplying congregations of Christians, clerical marriages flourished and families continued to add children to the faith. Jerome complained about bishops who "would not ordain men priests until they saw that their wives were well and truly pregnant."[12] To the extent that priests conformed to the Elvira canon, their wives were in a marriage situation like that of Mary, the mother of Jesus, whose husband Joseph was not a priest but who is revered as the protector of the holy family. Mary was wife and mother, maintaining the household and providing the ideal family life.

Persistence of Enkratism

Whether or not the decrees of the Council of Elvira received widespread notice, they are a signal that changes were taking place in the tradition of clergy marriages. In the Apostolic age, wives of clergy were revered and clergy marriage was affirmed. A gradual change was introduced into the concept of marriage as a "lower status" than virginity or celibacy. The asceticism of enkratism, or exaggerated abstinence, had not completely died out. St. Paul had already warned against false teachers who say that, "it is wrong to marry and to eat certain foods." (I Tim 4:3)

Tatian, who was condemned in 172, taught that it is sinful to eat meat, drink wine, and have sex relations.

Schillebeeckx notes that, "in the third and fourth centuries, enkratic tendencies became prominent. But now they caused the church fathers of the fourth century not only to begin a deeper theological consideration of religious celibacy, but also to defend more emphatically the goodness of the marriage state. On the other hand, it cannot be denied that a patristic exposition of marriage more often supported the Christian advantages of complete continence than it presented a reflection on marriage in itself."[13]

The rigoristic tendencies of enkratism, although limited to some fundamentalist sects, have never completely been eliminated among Roman Catholics. Christian asceticism, insofar as it is kept within the bounds of orthodoxy, still means penance, prayer and fasting. The ascetic tendencies begin to verge on heresy when they turn on sexuality as an intrinsic evil. There is no doubt that self-indulgence in the pleasures of the flesh and the gratification of the senses, are extensive in Western society. Yet, the virtues of self-control and continence are conscientiously practiced among both the celibate and the married. The concept of "cultic purity," reminiscent of the Levitical priesthood, suggested that the minister approaching the altar of sacrifice should refrain from marital coition. Insofar as they recognized a "model" in the Hebrew priesthood, Christian priests in many instances abstained from their wives before celebrating Mass.

Jean Galot points out that, "the function of the presbyter had been established in keeping with the Jewish model. It was exercised by married men, all the more so, since leadership in an established community was not likely to demand as much personal involvement as the itinerate apostolate in which Paul engaged."[14] There is much debate about the social and cultural evolution toward priestly celibacy. It is said that over the years the priesthood became "sacralized" as the performance of the sacred mysteries gradually became the exclusive function of certain men in the community. At the beginning of the third century "sexuality was disavowed on the ground that it was considered defiling and was believed to impinge adversely upon the sacred."

During the eight centuries between the Council of Elvira and the Council of Lateran, wives continued to live with their ordained husbands, although they were increasingly degraded and villified. Clerical marriages proliferated at all levels of the hierarchy, even while Church legislation was being introduced to diminish and sometimes punish it. The wives might be called "presbyterae," and "diaconissae," and official reforms were intermittently announced, but they refused to separate from their husbands. "In 745 Bishop Clement, born a Celt, had decided he could retain his grade of bishop, even though he had fathered two children before he had received this office." It is true that even "one of the Popes of that era, Adrian II (867-872), had been married before his election."[15]

Popes Had Children

Probably few contemporary Catholics are aware that there had been some Popes whose sons became Popes. The first of record is Anastasius I (399-401), whose son succeeded him as St. Innocent I (401-417). In the next century, Pope St. Hormisdas (514-523) begat his successor, the martyred St. Silverius (536-537); and four centuries later, Pope Sergius III (904-911) fathered Pope John XI (931-935). We know of one Pope, Theodore I (642-649), who was the son of a bishop. A number of other Roman Pontiffs were the sons of priests: St. Damasus I (366-384), St. Boniface I (418-422), St. Felix III (483-492), Anastasius II (496-498), St. Agapitus (535-536), Marinus I (882-884), and John XV (985-996). It is a regrettable omission of the historical records, that we know next to nothing about the mothers of these Popes.

We have been so preoccupied with celibacy and marriage among the Latin clergy that we neglect the importance of clergy wives in the Eastern Church where, as Vatican II observes, "there also exist married priests of outstanding merit." The sacred Synod intends in no way to change this ancient custom, but "it lovingly exhorts all those who have received the priesthood after marriage to persevere in their vocation." (*Presbyterorum Ordinis*, art. 16)

Perhaps it is helpful to recall that shortly after Elvira, and in another part of the Christian world, Bishop Paphnutius made his celebrated defense of clergy marriage. Constantelos says that, "until the first quarter of the sixth century there was no discrimination against married bishops and no distinction between married and unmarried candidates for the episcopate. In fact, there were canons protecting married bishops. For example, the fifth Apostolic canon states that any bishop (or presbyter or deacon) who dismisses his wife on account of piety [or on the pretension of piety] be defrocked or even excommunicated if he insists on doing so."[16]

One of the ironies of Church history is that we look in vain for an account of the life and works of the priest's wife, the central figure of all the arguments, debates and rules about the married clergy. What were the wives saying and doing during all these ecclesiastical controversies about their place in the Church of Christ? The wife was said to be the source and the cause of sexual impurity in her husband, and was villified as the seducer to evil. Such charges intensified over the centuries, although it is claimed that the tenth century was "the high point of clerical marriage in the Latin communion. Statistics, of course, are not available, but it is generally agreed that most rural priests were married, and that many urban clergy and bishops had wives and children."[17]

Stringent penalties were sometimes invoked against the clergymen who dared to marry, but attention must be paid to the wives who suffered even more severely. Henning said that the celibacy laws may have been hard on the priests, but "the cruelty leveled at their wives seems to have taken no end. There were laws which provided that a cleric may not visit his wife except in the presence of reliable witnesses. There were laws which imposed excommunication on those not ready to desert their wives. There were laws which threatened physical punishment to priests. Wives could even be sold! Did the women of those first ten centuries have an inkling that eventually they would be compromised to support the Church's idea of celibacy by these insidious means? What happened to their millions over the centuries?"[18]

While the lay people in the parishes seemed to have no reluctance to accept and admire the pastor's wife, the theologians and canonists frequently villified them. "Women were to be kept away from the male clerics, not only at home but also in church. An inherent male suspicion of women seems to underlie this disciplinary development and alongside it is a questionable theological image of women as inferior and secondary in creation."[19] The Church Fathers taught that women are inferior creatures and are responsible for the sin of the world. These vociferous anti-feminists degraded women who were to be kept away from the sacred ministers of the Church. When married men were ordained their wives were to be sent to a convent; any children born thereafter were illegitimate. According to the Gregorian reformers, "any sexual relationship between a cleric and a woman was fornication, while all clerical wives were concubines or worse, and the offspring of these unions were illegitimate."[20]

Celibacy and Abstinence

"What we have then," wrote Schillebeeckx, "is not a law of celibacy, but a law of abstinence connected with ritual purity, focused above all on the Eucharist. Despite this obligation to abstinence, married priests were forbidden to send away their wives; not only abstinence but also living together in love with his wife was an obligation for the priest under canon law."[21] This was not the interpretation of Peter Damian, perhaps the most violent opponent of clergy wives. He insisted that "contact with the female sex is the chief pollutant of clerical purity." He carried on his crusade through the pontificates of Leo IX (1048-1054), on to Gregory VII (1073-1085). Pope Leo declared clerical wives to be slaves of the Church, and Pope Urban offered these slaves to nobles who cooperated with clerical reform.

Barstow remarks: "It is not surprising that at this period one hears of desperate reactions on the part of the wives. When separated from their husbands some committed suicide while others physically attacked the bishops who tried to separate them. One, maddened by the destruction of her marriage, was said to have poisoned the wife of the lord who had forced her from her husband."[22]

Secular authorities were sometimes more censorious than their bishops. "In Normandy in 1080, Duke William, presiding over the Council of Lillebonne, criticized his bishops for not enforcing celibacy and warned that they must cease collecting *collagium*, the 'tax' married priests were forced to pay in order to live with their wives. Since the bishops had failed to purify the priesthood, William turned to the laity, setting up mixed courts of both clerical and lay jurors, to try clerics accused of concubinage."[23] In England, at the Second Reform Council of 1108, Anselm ruled that married clergy must give up their wives. The priests who refuse to repudiate their wives "and tried to remain in office by paying *collagium*, or by hiring substitutes, were allowed eight days in which to regularize their affairs. Recalcitrant priests were to be excommunicated, driven out by the laity and replaced by monks, their personal property confiscated by the bishop and their wives made chattels of the Church."[24]

Meanwhile, in the Eastern Church, the wives of clergy were treated with courtesy and Christian charity. "As late as the twelfth century there were married bishops (married laymen who upon ordination had refused to send their wives to convents as had been prescribed by the Council of Trullo, Canons 12 & 48). Emperor Isaac Angelus (1185-1195 and 1203-1204) issued a law against this practice. In the Eastern Church celibacy was never considered an obligatory prerequisite for the priesthood in any one of the priestly ranks. The canons did not impose upon or violate the free choice of the candidate for the priesthood."[25]

The so-called Gregorian Reform (1050-1250) was the most forceful and concerted effort by Church officials to remove the wives of clergy and to promote only bachelors to holy orders.

There were, however, the continuing practical problems of supporting the ex-wives and the children of clergy. Coriden opines that "the most radical single piece of legislation in this long history was that enacted by the Second Lateran Council in 1139 (and reiterated at Lateran IV in 1215) which declared the marriages of clergy to be null and void—no marriages at all; previously they were simply considered to be illicit, illegal."[26]

From this point on, the women who continued to marry priests were declared to be in an invalid relationship. In the language of the Church they were now concubines, which means that clerical celibacy was far from firmly established. As Coriden says, "certainly concubinage continued to be a serious problem up to and through the Reformation and Counter-Reformation periods."

It was during the Reformation period, however, that the status of married Christian women was raised, but not among Catholics. Luther and Calvin argued that marriage was preferable to celibacy on biblical grounds. "The honor accorded to marriage in both Lutheran and Calvinist circles had an impact on the status of women. Since sexuality was no longer viewed as evil, the married woman at least was not cast in the role of temptress and seducer." Of course, the ordained leaders among the Reformers, many of them celibate monks, "entered into marriage and urged other celibate Christians to do the same. Priests serving the newly formed congregations were encouraged to take wives."[27]

Clergy marriage among the Reformers "meant a new sphere of activity for some women as 'ministers'' wives." These women often "found themselves presiding over households that were the centers of cultural and intellectual activities. They offered hospitality to theologians, advice to other clergy, and bed and board to young students. Luther's wife, Katherine von Bora, presided over barnyard, fish pond, orchard, a host of servants, children, sick visitors, student boarders, church leaders, and theologians."[28] Women "were not denounced as seducers and corrupters in the Lutheran and Calvinist literature and they were not treated with scorn and derision. Calvin objected to the vulgar expression that women were a 'necessary evil,' while Luther took a stand against those who 'despised the female sex.'"

The Finality of Trent

The Council of Trent (1545-1563) was the organized Roman response to the Protestant Reformation. It confirmed the "invalidating aspect of Sacred Orders" in respect to marriage. It went even further and into the area of personal opinion by declaring that, "If anyone says the marriage state excels the state of virginity or celibacy, or that it is better and happier to be united in matrimony than to remain in virginity or celibacy, let him be anathema." (Session 24, Canon 10) The prohibition against clerical marriage was now firmly established, which meant that any woman who attempted marriage with a clergyman had to settle for invalid (and immoral) marital relations. These prohibitions continued through and beyond the First Vatican Council in 1870, where the authority of the Roman Church was strengthened with the doctrine of papal infallibility.

Added to the status of invalid marriage was the declaration of sacrilege in the 1918 Code of Canon Law, which stated that "clerics in major orders (subdiaconate, diaconate, priesthood) are prevented from marrying and so obliged to observe chastity that those sinning against it are also guilty of sacrilege." (CIC 132) The law was expanded further, with prohibitions that removed temptations against the priest's vow of chastity. Rectory housekeepers must be beyond the age of suspicion, and priests must avoid association with women who may compromise them. In the *Lex Sacri Coelibatus* of 1936, we note that clerics in sacred orders who get married in a civil ceremony are *ipso facto* excommunicated.

Clara Henning says that, "if life were simple and love an uninviting pastime, we might be able to regard celibacy as a charming idiosyncracy of Catholic culture. But life is complex and love a universal need. Consequently, a simple law, like Canon 132 which prohibits priests from marrying, cannot stand on its own authority; it must be assisted by complementary regulations such as the insulting and suggestive Canon 133." She thinks that "celibacy" has always been a threatening term. "We have further always viewed celibacy as primarily the priests' problem; after all, they have to live it. Celibacy is very much a woman's problem. This innocuous term has over the centuries created a multitude of evils, most of which prove to be particularly insulting and generally detrimental to women."[29]

The history of clerical wives has necessarily been associated with the history of clerical celibacy. After all, the prohibition against married priests is intimately and immediately the prohibition against priests' wives. The Canon Law continues to promote celibacy while grudgingly the Vatican makes some exception for clergy couples converting from other Christian denominations, and a much larger concession to the ordination of married deacons. Women are not allowed to marry ordained men, but married women are allowed to remain wives of men who are ordained in holy orders.

In our own times, the feminist movement promotes the ordination of women to the priesthood while continuing also to support the movement of the married priesthood. It is likely that permission will be given for a married priesthood before the Vatican allows the ordination of women. In Christian history there have been many instances of married priests, but the ordination of women to the priesthood is a completely strange innovation. "In this time of transition," writes James Coriden, "the entire Church must be prepared for the acceptance of the ministry of married priests." Furthermore, "the faithful should see in the married priest and his wife an example of marriage in Christ."[30]

Endnotes

1. *The Apocryphal Gospel*, known as *Protoevangelium Jacobi*, fabricated a biography of Mary's parents around 175 A.D.

2. Elisabeth Moltmann-Wendel, *Liberty, Equality, Sisterhood,* Philadelphia, Fortress, 1978, p. 23, writes of "women of the earliest Church who were leaders of congregations meeting in homes. But we must not think of them as housewives in a modern family."

3. Daniel J. Harrington, *God's People in Christ,* Philadelphia, Fortress Press, 1980, p. 30.

4. Wayne A. Meeks, *The First Urban Christians,* New Haven, Yale University Press, 1983, p. 75. See also, "The House Church," pp. 175-184, in Elisabeth Schussler-Fiorensa, *In Memory of Her,* New York, Crossroad, 1983.

5. Edward Schillebeeckx, *The Church with a Human Face,* New York, Crossroad, 1985, p. 46. It was not till the fourth century that "it became possible to have separate church buildings," p. 47.

6. Edward Schillebeeckx, *Celibacy,* New York, Sheed & Ward, 1968, pp. 20-21.

7. Jean-Paul Audet, *Structures of Christian Priesthood,* New York, Macmillan, 1968, p. 19.

8. Raymond Brown, *The Churches the Apostles Left Behind,* New York, Paulist Press, 1984, p. 34.

9. Julia O'Faolain and Lauro Martines, *Not in God's Image; Women in History,* London, Virago, 1979, p. 88.

10. Demetrios Constantelos, "Marriage and Celibacy of the Clergy in the Orthodox Church," pp. 30-38, in William Bassett and Peter Huizing, eds., *Celibacy in the Church,* New York, Herder & Herder, 1972.

11. Joseph H. Fichter, *Saint Cecil Cyprian,* St. Louis, Herder, 1942, pp. 6-7.

12. Peter Brown, *The Body and Society,* New York, Columbia University, 1988, p. 358.

13. Schillebeeckx, *Celibacy, op. cit.,* p. 29.

14. Jean Galot, *Theology of the Priesthood,* San Francisco, Ignatius Press, 1985, p. 240.

15. Anne L. Barstow, *Married Priests and the Reforming Papacy*, Lewiston, Edwin Mellen, 1982, p. 35.

16. Constantelos, *op. cit,* p. 33.

17. Barstow, *op. cit.*, p. 37.

18. Clara Maria Henning, "Celibacy as a Feminist Issue," pp. 87-104, in Robert Heyer, ed., *Women and Orders,* New York, Paulist Press, 1974.

19. Francine Cardman, "Women, Ordination and Tradition," *Commonweal,* December 17, 1976, pp. 807-810.

20. Barstow, *op. cit.*, p. 5.

21. Edward Schillebeeckx, *The Church with a Human Face,* New York, Crossroad, 1985, p. 242.

22. Barstow, *op. cit.*, p. 83.

23. *Ibid.*, p. 89.

24. *Ibid.*, p. 92.

25. Constantelos, *op. cit.*, p. 35.

26. James A. Coriden, "Celibacy, Canon Law and Synod 1971," pp. 109-124, in Bassett and Huizing, *op. cit.*

27. Barbara J. MacHaffie, *Her Story: Women in Christian Tradition,* Philadelphia, Fortress Press, 1986, pp. 62f.

28. *Ibid.*, p. 63.

29. Henning, *op. cit.*, pp. 88f.

30. Coriden, *op. cit.*, p. 122.

Chapter Two

Women in Ministry

Although, ultimately, women were canonically prohibited from sharing bed and board with ordained clergy in the Latin Church, they were seen everywhere in the New Testament as the firmest believers in Jesus. Jean Danielou remarks that, "all Christian history—and particularly in the first centuries—shows that women have played a considerable part in missionary work, in worship and in teaching."[1] We have learned hardly anything about their roles as the wives and mothers in priestly families, but there is overwhelming evidence that the bulk of Christian ministry has been carried by the women.

Occasionally we celebrate saintly "women of the world," like Helena, the mother of Constantine; Monica, mother of Augustine; Bridget, queen of Sweden. We know even more about "women of the Church," like Catherine of Siena, Theresa of Avila, Therese of Lisieux. Nevertheless, we are forced to agree with Ursula King, when she says that, "wherever one looks in the world, religious institutions are dominated by men. Women are largely invisible, or at least marginal, to the public positions of power, authority and hierarchy. There are hardly ever official 'spokeswomen' of religious institutions; whereas, at the grassroots level, women everywhere form a majority of participants in ordinary day-to-day religious life."[2]

In the logic of the Jewish culture which prevailed among the early Christians, women were expected always to play a secondary role. The extent to which Jesus disregarded this demeaning custom is frequently pointed out by commentators of the Bible. Indeed, the Gospel of Luke is the best demonstration of Jesus' regard for women. Swidler has counted forty-two passages in Luke, dealing with women, as compared to only eight in the

Gospel of John.[3] It has even been suggested that the author of Luke's gospel could have been a woman.

Ecclesial Women

Besides Mary, whose exalted status is not questioned by even the most fiery feminist, homage is due Elizabeth, before the birth of Christ, and Mary Magdalene, at the death of Christ. Martha and her sister Mary were personal friends of Jesus. During His lifetime there were many women to whom Jesus ministered, like Peter's mother-in-law, the widow of Naim, the woman taken in adultery, the penitent woman at the Pharisee's dinner. In all probability, women were present at the Last Supper, at which they were served by men. In this case, says E. Jane Via, "the roles are reversed. The men serve the women and Jesus acts as waiter."[4]

The twelve apostles did not include a woman, but in the larger fellowship of Christ's disciples women certainly outnumbered men. After Pentecost, and even at the beginning of Apostolic times, there is much evidence of zealous women spreading the Gospel message of Jesus, evangelizing converts, anointing the women at baptism. Paul speaks of women praying and telling God's message along with men in public worship. (I Cor. 11:5) Biblical experts continue to assemble New Testament evidence that "many of the functions which were later associated with the priestly ministry were, in fact, exercised by women." Furthermore, "the claim that the intention and example of Jesus, and the example of the Apostles provide a norm excluding women from priestly ministry, cannot be sustained on either logical or historical grounds."[5]

For want of a better term, the women we here designate as "ecclesial" were devoted members of the Church community, were recognized by the clergy leaders—bishops and priests—but had no characteristics of monastic cloister. They continued in the "midst of the world," serving the Church and its people. They were not anchorites who may have gone off to their solitary hermitage. Nor did they belong to the vast category of the wives of clergy, about whom there is little historical record.

They lived in "open" communities and in spiritual relationship with the bishop. They were not "clerical" in the sense of ordination. Their nearest equivalent in modern society is probably the "secular institute," approved by Pope Pius XII in 1947.

One may suggest that the life-style of these ecclesial women developed as an alternative to the clerical life-style of male Christians. They were not allowed ordination, even in the primitive sense of that term, at the time of the Apostles. The three recognizable female ecclesial categories were institutional "orders" of widows, virgins and deaconesses. Their functional ministry was guided by the Spirit in the early Church, before any thought was given to rules and constitutions. They were not intended in any way to be an organization separate from the emerging ecclesiastical structure; yet, they were neither ordained clerics nor the wives of clerics.[6]

There is no suggestion that these groups of Christian women deliberately set themselves apart from the male leadership of the Church, or thought of themselves as feminists or liberationists. Patriarchy, or male domination, was simply a given of the Jewish culture. These ecclesial women accepted Jesus and His teaching as a gift for all humanity, which they could help to propagate under the given circumstances. As far as we know and can tell at this distance in time, neither organized feminism nor anti-feminism existed among the early Christians. We do not know whether they gave a new interpretation to Paul's declaration of equality between the sexes, which meant that the salvation of Jesus, and the work of the Spirit, were for the benefit of all.

The Order of Widows

The earliest groups of ecclesial women to whom attention was given were those of widows and they were first mentioned as the recipients of Christian welfare benefits. An ethnic confrontation between the Greek-speaking and the Hebrew-speaking Christians was voiced in the complaint that the widows of the Greek group were not given their share in the distribution of benefits. (Acts 6:1) In the Gospel narratives, widows are often seen as poor and needy. The widow who dropped two copper coins in the Temple treasury was "poor." (Mark 12:41) The widows had benefited from the "shirts and coats" Dorcas had made for them. (Acts 9:39)

Paul takes time to tell Timothy how widows should be treated in age categories: "Do not add any widow to the list of widows unless she is more than sixty years old." Younger widows should not be put on the list because they may decide to remarry or waste their time as "gossips and busybodies." Otherwise, the widows should be cared for by their relatives; the burden should not be put on the Church, so that "it may take care of the widows who are all alone." (I Tim. 5) Paul wants the family, the children and grandchildren, to take care of their widows. If they fail in this duty, they "are worse than unbelievers."

In his first letter to Timothy, Paul seems to be laying down a simple "rule of life" for the *ordo* of widows, while recognizing them as a distinct group of believers. Even though the "true widow" is now in need and has no one to care for her, she hopes in God and continues to pray night and day. She has a "reputation for good deeds, brought up her children well, received strangers in her home, washed the feet of God's people, helped those in trouble, and gave herself to all kinds of good works." (I Tim. 5)

The complaints about the discriminatory treatment of Hellenic widows were a symptom of ethnic differences among the early Christians. The basic question that led to the argument between Peter and Paul at the so-called Council of Jerusalem was whether the gentile converts to Christ had to follow the Mosaic customs on circumcision, dietary rules, and other Jewish mores. These disputes were settled amicably when the Apostles and elders, together with the whole church, wrote to the Gentile Christians, "For the Holy Spirit and we have agreed not to put any other burden on you besides these necessary rules." (Acts 15:28)

It should be noted that this dispute about preferential treatment of Aramaic widows over Hellenic widows was the occasion for the institution of the diaconate. Of course, the needs of Christians were not limited to those of widows. The Apostles asked the brothers to choose men who "are known to be full of the Holy Spirit and wisdom." The whole group then chose Stephen and six other worthy men and presented them to the Apostles "who prayed and placed their hands on them." (Acts 6:6) Thus, the deacons were officially instituted and approved. "It was one of the main tasks of these gifted deacons to officiate at the daily *diakonia*, a service for the widows of Apostolic institutions, under the direction of the Apostles. Their task was to form by their leadership and instruction an elite group of women for the service of the Church."[6]

While the indigence of the widows was the occasion for the selection of deacons, who in turn led to the institution of the order of widows, the fact is that the widows themselves came to be the chief caretakers for needy Christians. At first, they had been mainly the recipients of charity, but as they grew and added prosperous widows to the membership, many of them became themselves the dispensers of charity. Some of these consecrated women were "rich widows" who could easily distribute their surplus funds and encourage others to do the same. The widow Tabitha, for whom Peter was called to Joppa, had widow friends who apparently shared her way of life. (Acts 9:35)

It appears that the widows continued to share with deacons the kinds of "social work" needed among the early Christians. They apparently did not share with deacons the liturgical functions of the Church, "but they were publicly and officially enrolled in the order of widows after a suitable period of testing." They remained unmarried but were probably not called upon to vow themselves to celibacy. Schneiders thinks that, "their decision not to remarry was partly motivated by the generally negative view of second marriages in the early Church but, since such marriages were not forbidden, their choice of celibacy was deliberate and free."[7]

From an institutional perspective, the widows were the first to be recognized. While they were not ordained and could not be included among the clergy, they were listed in the *Apostolic Tradition* immediately after the deacons. They were certainly the oldest of the orders of women in the Church. "In the third century the position of the widows reached its highest point. Their position was official; they constituted an 'order'; they were part of the hierarchy. Yet, because their ministry was not a liturgical one, their position was not clerical."[8]

The Order of Virgins

As the numbers and prestige of consecrated widows began to decline, more attention was paid to the prominence of female virgins. Although the virgin females became a kind of prototype in Christian literature, virginity is the virtuous status of both sexes. In the middle of the second century the martyr Justin points with pride to the "many men and women, sixty and seventy years old who, imbued from childhood with the teaching of Christ, keep their integrity."[9] Paul was talking about male virgins, or celibates, when he took up the matter of the unmarried. "Considering the present distress, I think it is better for a man to stay as he is." This is for the personal benefit of the male. "I would like you to be free from worry. An unmarried man concerns himself about the Lord's work, because he is trying to please the Lord." (I Cor. 7:32)

In the early Christian society, influenced by the culture mores of Judaism, the expected pattern was marriage and the production of children. Virginity was not highly favored among the Jews and there appears to be little emphasis on it among the Jewish converts to Christianity. In other words, if a person wanted to remain virginal for the sake of the Gospel, it was a private decision. Unlike widowhood, virginity was not institutionalized, either in Judaism or early Christianity. In Rome, at the same time, the Vestal Virgins were held in high regard, were organized and regularized.

The female who assumed the obligations of virginity did so at her own volition and not in a solemn ceremonial act, as was the case with the organized widows. While the virgin may have been honored among the early Christians and could be called an ecclesial woman in function of her membership in the Christian community, she was not committed to any specific social or personal role. In those early years there were no congregations of virgins set apart for the service of God or for the ministry of the people. "Here was a private choice, not of service in general, but of a specific and beautiful form of spiritual service—the ascetical witness of the sheer fact of virginity." Simply by being what she was, "for the sake of the kingdom of heaven, she served the Church."[10] Her spirit of asceticism was distinct from that of the widow.

It was not until the third century that the virgins gained recognition as an organized group. "They must have met frequently," writes McKenna, "or there would have been little point in St. Cyprian's exhortation to the older virgins 'to give instruction to the younger,' and to the younger to 'encourage those of your own age,' and to all of them to 'stimulate one another by mutual words of encouragement, and summon each other to glory by rival proofs of virtue.'"[11]

It has been noted that celibacy and virginity gave Christian women a voluntary option other than marriage and motherhood. Domesticity was the only "career" available to women in the ancient world. "The virginal life, on the other hand, freed women from the cycle of childbearing and dependence upon men."[12] McKenna adds that, "virgins were succeeding to the functions as well as to the honors traditionally assigned to the widows and deaconesses. Clement's advice to the virgins was to seek their sanctification in the service of their neighbors and in apostolic activity in the bosom of the Christian communities."[13]

Historians suggest that virginal asceticism came into vogue when the peace of Constantine put an end to the era of martyrs. Virginity became a recognized way of life, even for women who did not retire to the convent. "The virgins under Ambrose's direction seem to have resided with their families, since no convents appear to have existed in Milan."[14] Over the centuries the consecrated virgins living in monasteries outnumbered those living in the world, until Lateran II, in 1139, abolished the rite of consecration outside the cloister. This was still the case as late as 1950, when Pius XII reiterated in his document, *Sponsa Christi*, that the rite of consecration was reserved solely for cloistered nuns.

As in so many aspects of the *aggiornamento*, the Second Vatican Council called for the revision of the liturgical rite for the consecration of virgins (*Sacrosanctum Concilium*, art. 80) The specifics of this "state of life" were spelled out in the revised Code of Canon Law of 1982. When the diocesan bishops consecrate them according to the approved liturgical rite, they are "mystically espoused to Christ and dedicated to the service of the Church." (Canon 604) The consecration is sacramental, not a sacrament, and if the woman continues to "live in the world," it establishes "no claim to maintenance, employment or revenue from the diocese."[15]

In the early centuries the virgins were the forerunners of the large numbers of women who began to associate in religious communities and to parallel the monastic orders of men religious. Georges Tavard asks the question: "Once a woman entered the way of life of virginity she was counted among the ascetics, frequented the sacred liturgy assiduously, and conversed on biblical matters; what difference remained between her and a monk?" Some Christians apparently thought that asceticism equalized the sexes, and that the difference of sex could safely be ignored. There arose then the phenomenon of women *agapetai*, called in Latin, *virgines subintroductae*, who were not always required to live in cloister. "There were unmarried deacons, priests, monks, and even bishops, who shared their living quarters" with these women consecrated to virginity.[16] St. Jerome condemned this as a scandalous practice. In his letter to Eustochium he wrote, "they occupy the same room and often the same bed, and yet, they call us suspicious if we think that anything is wrong."[17]

The Order of Deaconesses

Widows and virgins were actively engaged in the early ministry among the followers of Christ, but there is only one mention of a deaconess when Paul commended to the Roman community, "our sister Phoebe," who served the Church in Conchreae. (Rom. 16:1) Luke tells us that when Jesus went through the towns and villages, preaching the good news about the Kingdom of God, he was accompanied not only by the twelve apostles but by Mary, Joanna, Suzanna, and "many other women who helped Jesus with their belongings." (Luke 8:1-3) Martimort warns us that it would be "gratuitous" to suppose that Luke was thinking of these women as deaconesses because women were never ordained and deaconesses did not appear until the third century.[18]

In some relatively unorganized fashion, "their beginnings stemmed back to apostolic times," writes Jean Danielou. "But it was in the third century that this order became important and replaced that of widows; it was linked to the deacons, and through them to the bishop. The most notable evidence of this promotion of the deaconesses is the *Didascalia Apostolorum*. The deaconesses are a parallel order with the deacons; they replace the latter in ministering to women, visiting the sick, baptismal anointing. The deaconess must look after women neophytes, instruct them and encourage them. There seems, at this period, to have been an ordination of deaconesses with a laying-on of hands."[19]

The deaconess order did not evolve in strict continuity out of the Rome-Jerusalem axis, but seems to have been an invention of the Church in Syria. From there it extended throughout the East. It was not the replication and "upgrading" of the ministry of widows and virgins and other pious women during the generation following Pentecost. The hierarchy, as it came to be recognized in later years, seemed to embrace only male clergy, but the office of deaconess made way for women during the period when the minor orders were introduced. In descending order of importance then, we recognize bishops, presbyters, deacons, deaconesses, lectors, ministers, subdeacons, cantors, and porters. "Below the doorkeepers," writes Danielou, "were the gravediggers who for quite some time were included among the clerics. On the other hand, bodies (*ordines*) of widows, of consecrated virgins, and of deaconesses, had a status which set them apart from simple lay people."[20]

The segregation of the sexes, especially in liturgical and spiritual activities which was characteristic of the Jewish tradition, had carried over to the Christian community. Thus, it was to be expected that deacons ministered to males, while deaconesses ministered to females. Both, of course, were assistants to the bishop in carrying out his comprehensive duties. The dispute about the existence and function of deaconesses seems to center on their inclusion into the hierarchical order. There appears to be no dispute that men were "raised" by holy orders to the status of permanent deacon. The masculine argument was (and continues to be) that women simply cannot be ordained, that they are not fit subjects to receive the sacrament of holy orders. Neither the order of widows nor the order of virgins was considered ready for ordination, even at the lowest level of the clerical hierarchy.

Perhaps the most famous of the deaconesses was Olympias, who was born in Constantinople in 368. She was a friend of St. John Chrysostom, who addressed seventeen epistles to her. She was praised by Gregory of Nyssa, and well acquainted with Gregory of Nazianzen. Olympias was a young widow when Bishop Nectarius ordained her to the diaconate. "She built a hospital-hospitality house in Constantinople and gathered other young women to serve in it. These women lived a monastic life together with Olympias and other deaconesses who had been ordained by Chrysostom."[21]

In an effort to disprove the ordination of deaconesses, or at least to prove that deacons were ordained differently from deaconesses, Martimort argues: (a) That deaconesses did not receive the *orarion* over their shoulders, but rather around their necks, with the two ends hanging down in front; (b) the deaconess did not genuflect or rest her head against the altar; (c) she did not receive the *rhipidion* because she could not serve Mass;

(d) they were never given grounds to hope, as deacons were, that they might aspire to the priesthood; and (e) "the bishop prays, putting his hand on her head, but not as for ordination, but for a benediction."[22]

Women in Holy Orders

The concept of ordination is commonly focused on the sacrament of Holy Orders, which is bestowed only on males in the tradition of the Church. The functions of the sacerdotal office may be performed only by priests, and Danielou declares that, "There has never been any mention of women filling strictly sacerdotal offices. We never see a woman offering the Eucharistic Sacrifice, or ordaining, or preaching, in the Church." He complains that, "the status of the ministry exercised by women has never been clearly defined. Sometimes it has been integrated into the ordained ministry and sometimes it has been regarded as a lay ministry."[23]

Women who engaged in the Christian ministry were always under the jurisdiction of the male episcopacy and performed their duties alongside clerical males. The "orders" of virgins and of widows were composed of women who were assigned, appointed, and even consecrated, but they did not become ordained clergy, even when they experienced the laying-on of hands by the bishop. In the case of the diaconate, Danielou has no hesitation to say that their ordination "makes them into an actual minor order." He quotes the particular ordination formula: "Thou shalt lay thy hands upon her in the presence of the Presbyters, the Deacons, and the Deaconesses." The prayer is then made to God with the petition: "Look upon thy servant chosen for the ministry (*diakonia*) and give to her the Holy Spirit that she may worthily perform the office committed unto her."[24]

One of the more spectacular examples of women's "ordination" is the medieval enthronement of quasi-episcopal abbesses. In some instances, a man could be the head, or abbot, of a religious congregation without having been ordained to the priesthood. Neither St. Benedict nor St. Francis was in holy orders, nor were they raised to the episcopacy. Nor did the jurisdiction of an abbess comprise the sacerdotal powers of a bishop. "Such functions as the ordaining of priests, the dedication and consecration of altars, the blessing of the chrismatory oils, were reserved to the specific sacerdotal power of the bishop alone."[25] "What is meant by quasi-episcopal jurisdiction is that the abbess, like the abbot, "had the same duties and rights to act within their separated territories belonging to the congregation as had a bishop within his diocese."[26]

Joan Morris rightly claims to have revealed the "Hidden History of Women with Clerical Ordination and the Jurisdiction of Bishops." The focus of her historical research is on the status and role of the abbess, an office that flourished in the Church for a thousand years. She argues in a kind of feminist polemic that the abbess was genuinely consecrated and privileged to preach, read the Gospel, hear the confessions of nuns. "It was only in the sixteenth century that an anti-feminist attitude arose with regard to the jurisdiction of abbesses and that it became a subject of debate; whereas, before it had not been questioned."[27] It was finally the Council of Trent that undermined the status of the abbess, mainly on the basis of their exclusion from priestly ordination.

Cloistered Women

In the early centuries of the Church there were probably some saintly women who went to live in the solitude of the desert and perhaps associated with other women, but we have little reliable information about female anchorites and cenobites till generations later. The ecclesial women we discuss here were not monastic or cloistered. Recognized and appreciated as widows, virgins and deaconesses, they were accorded special status within the Christian community. The first official move towards the common life of the cloister for women was made in the year 358, by St. Macrina, the sister of St. Basil. It was also in the fourth century that St. Jerome, who had experimented with the hermit's life for a few years in the desert, became the foremost advocate of ascetic celibacy for women.

Jerome, who, like his contemporary, St. Augustine, had lost his virginity in youth, wrote notoriously misogynist treatises and letters. Despite this male chauvinism, he seemed to have a strong attraction to women. "During his stay in Rome, he acquired a circle of wealthy Roman women among his devotees."[28] As a matter of record, "some of them followed him to Bethlehem and set up a convent near the male monastic institution he established there." The conventual life, for women as well as for men, was first regularized in 451 at the Council of Chalcedon. The best-known and most imitated monastic instructions were the Rule of Benedict of Nursia who in 510, with his sister Scholastica, established separate convents, or abbeys, for females.

The cloistered nuns differed radically from the three types of ecclesial women we discussed above. These women of the early Christian communities practically disappeared from Church history about the fifth century and were replaced by cloistered contemplatives until the sixteenth century. "Physical separation from the world, and in particular from the opposite sex, is an ancient ascetic discipline common to males and females. In the early sixth century, Bishop Caesarius of Arles incorporated that custom into his rule for nuns. The practice was gradually extended for reasons of physical safety as well as ascetic discipline. Both Dominic and Francis founded second orders for women, but ecclesial practice required that these women be cloistered. Although the stringency of the cloister varied, in effect the active side of the mendicant charism was excluded."[29]

Even during those centuries it is questionable that inviolable cloister was essential to the monastic vocation. Papal cloister was not strictly imposed until the Council of Trent in the sixteenth century, and then for women only. It was fairly common for a nun to be absent from the convent for approved reasons.[30] A better-known exception was the growth of the Beguines in the thirteenth century, a group who "occupied a position midway between monastic and lay states." They devoted themselves to good works, like teaching and nursing, and supported themselves with manual work. Although sometimes suspected of heresy, they also gained informal papal approval. They were the medieval forerunners of secular institutes which obtained papal recognition only in 1947.[31]

The tendency toward enkratism, which had not been present in Apostolic times, or in the early centuries, developed with the expansion of monasticism. The practice of the evangelical counsels of poverty, chastity and obedience suggested that the monastic life was a higher way and that the celibate state was essentially superior to the married state. It became increasingly important that dedicated virginal women keep away from males. The law of enclosure means that the religious residence is reserved for the exclusive use of the nuns who belong to the congregation. The earliest religious women in the monastic tradition were contemplative nuns, whose rule of enclosure was strict. Later congregations of religious women were for the most part semi-cloistered, which allowed them to participate in the active ministry. Even so, their residence was not open to lay people, especially males.

The typical hierarchical organization of the Latin Church is reflected in the differential status of the nuns, who were divided into professed of solemn vows and of simple vows, into choir sisters and extern sisters. The Apostolic Constitution, *Sponsa Christi,* says that the papal cloister must be "observed in all monasteries of nuns, either in its major form when the nuns take solemn vows and lead an exclusively contemplative life; or, in the form of minor enclosure when a notable number of the nuns, even though bound by solemn vows, regularly engage in some compatible activity; or, by special permission of the Holy See, take simple vows but lead only a contemplative life." (art. 3, 2)

Religious Sisters

During the early Reformation, attempts were made to "activate" the cloistered monks and nuns. The Barnabites and the Jesuits were the first to establish non-cloistered communities of men with solemn vows, in the conviction that contemplative spirituality could be combined with apostolic spirituality. They encountered considerable opposition from conservative prelates, who were even more strongly opposed to Mary Ward, who "wanted a group of uncloistered nuns without any distinctive habit, bound together by their vow and their rule, and under a superior general with authority to transfer the sisters. Mary's ideas were regarded as dangerously novel, and their Ignatian spirit aroused the anti-Jesuits."[32] The "novelties" of this Sisterhood were suppressed by Pope Urban VIII, in 1631, but the community survived and is now known as the "Ladies of Loretto." Similar adaptations were attempted but thwarted in the founding of the Ursulines and the Sisters of the Visitation. The Daughters of Charity, with the help of Vincent de Paul, succeeded in remaining both active and uncloistered, by refusing to take solemn perpetual vows. They are not canonically defined as religious but are members of a "society of common life."

For more than a thousand years the term, "religious" was reserved mainly to celibate women and men contemplatives who lived in perpetual *clausura*. Cardinal Suenens remarked that, "a religious was by origin and by definition an enclosed person taking solemn vows. The idea of unenclosed nuns seemed something unholy."[33] Many women who felt called to serve God and the Church in a more flexible manner were deterred by the rigidities and restrictions of convent life, that could be changed only with the approval of the Apostolic See, through the Office of the Sacred Congregation for Religious. Yet, in America the activist orders grew the most rapidly.

American Sisters realized that the restrictions and inhibitions of bygone centuries were no longer practical in the modern age. They had roughed it as missionaries on the frontier, worked in primitive clinics and hospitals, took care of the needy and the unfortunate, taught the children of immigrants; indeed, had done every kind of active social ministry. All the while they sustained themselves spiritually in their virtuous lives of prayer, self-denial and contemplation. During the first half of this century in America, religious orders of women were increasing rapidly in membership and were multiplying their high schools and colleges, hospitals and social agencies. The need for professional training in all these fields was becoming more urgent.

The American religious orders of women had already been pressing for change, moving towards the professionalization of their apostolic ministries, when Pope Pius XII in 1950 took the first steps toward modernization. In the following year (1951) the First International Congress of Religious Teaching Sisters met in Rome. The Pope advised them to modernize their apparel, get rid of outmoded customs and rules and, above all, give the Sisters professional training that "corresponds in quality and academic degrees" to their lay contemporaries.[34]

Perhaps without realizing it, the Pope was confirming the analysis that the American Sisters themselves had been developing over recent decades. Some of them had already received doctoral degrees at Catholic University, at Fordham, Marquette, Notre Dame, and St. Louis Universities. From a functional perspective, the Sisters wanted to alter their life-styles, their customs and rules, in order to perform more efficiently the good works they were destined to do.

Many of the Sisters themselves now claim that the change of structures has required a more authentic, contemplative and communal dimension to their modern apostolate. They argue that the American Sisterhoods knew where they were going, and were well on the way, even before the opening of the Second Vatican Council in 1962. Among the sixteen major documents issuing from the Council, the principal one pertaining to the modernization of the Sisterhoods was the Decree on "The Appropriate Renewal of the Religious Life," (*Perfectae Caritatis*) of 28 October, 1965. By that time, John XXIII was deceased, and the document was issued over the signature of his successor, Paul VI.

The Decree recommends renewal of spirituality and adaptation of ministries. These recommendations were not to be put into effect until the Pope could state the norms for the implementation of change. He did this with an apostolic letter, *Ecclesiae Sanctae,* in the following year. Each congregation had to convene a general chapter within three years, with extensive and open consultation among all members. They were urged to revise their constitutions and make all the adaptations they considered necessary. The period of experimentation was adjudged completed when the religious orders submitted their revised constitutions to Roman authorities, which most of them did by 1970.

Vatican Recall

It appears that response from Rome was deliberately delayed until the new Canon Law was promulgated in January, 1983. The arrival of a new Pope, John Paul II, in 1978, whose conservative preferences soon became known, was an added delay. This means that the process of renewal, which began for the Sisters in the early 1950's, was still without papal approval. With the promulgation of the new Code of Canon Law, the modernity of the Sisters' renewal collided with the traditions of the Vatican. Instead of responding to the Sisters' renewal programs, the Pope, in 1983, appointed a committee of American Bishops to assist the active religious orders to "live their ecclesial vocation to the full."

At the same time, there came a document from the Sacred Congregation for Religious and Secular Institutes, which spelled out the "Essential Elements in the Church Teaching on Religious Life."[35] These fundamental norms, as taken from the revised Code of Canon Law, were meant to be the final word in the renewal process of the religious congregations. Not only was the "experiment" terminated, it had all been in vain, and all the programs worked out by the Sisters for the *aggiornamento* of their communities were bluntly repudiated. The startling message from the Vatican was that the Sisterhoods must return to the traditional definition of religious life. They were to wear a specific religious garb, observe a common life by returning to their convents, pronounce the public vows of poverty, chastity and obedience, and restrict their apostolic ministries to those that are "proper" to their institute.

There can be no doubt that the specific target of this directive from the Sacred Congregation was the active American Sisterhood. It is addressed to "institutes dedicated to apostolic works" and not to the religious communities of contemplative nuns. The enormous efforts that went into three decades of renewal and experimentation were dismissed in favor of the unchanging traditional criteria of religious life. The rationale for this decision was neither contemporary nor existential. It was argued that, "historical and cultural changes bring about evolution in the lived reality, but the forms and direction which the evolution takes are determined by the essential elements without which religious life loses its identity." This means that in the long run, the basis for renewal and adaptation is not to be the "lived reality" of the Sisters themselves, but the preordained determinations of the Vatican prelates.

The speculation persists that Pope John Paul II was determined to "rein in" the American religious women who are generally recognized as the most progressive Catholic Sisterhood in the world. The Vatican document seems to be saying that the renewal efforts over these three decades were not really "religious." Since they have gone "too far," they must be brought back under the hierarchical system which prevailed in previous centuries; but it is not likely that the developed ministries of the American Sisters will be brought to a standstill, or that the clock of progress can be turned back thirty years. Among the Sisters themselves there is the conviction that a thirteenth-century life-style cannot be re-fashioned for their twentieth-century responsibilities. One of the outspoken commentators feels that the letter on the Essential Elements is a "feeble recall to a lukewarm monastic life-style completely divorced from Vatican II ideology."[36]

Instead of the traditional humble and submissive acceptance of Vatican paternalism, the American Sisters have reacted in two ways: The first was the enormous exodus from the religious Sisterhoods. Thousands of religious women simply resigned from the religious vocation. Those who stayed responded in ways least expected by the Vatican. As Ann Ware wrote, "Sisters donned street clothes, took jobs on public university campuses, managed housing developments, stood on picket lines, or ran for public office."[37] Perhaps unexpectedly, the ministerial activities of the Sisters expanded enormously within the Church. Earning master's degrees in theological seminaries, they found employment as pastoral associates, liturgists and directors of religious education. They trained in clinical pastoral education and moved from nursing to hospital chaplaincy. With preparation in spiritual and psychological guidance, many Sisters conduct retreats for the laity. They are assisting, and in some instances replacing, the clergy in campus ministry. It is not unusual now to find Sisters at work in chancery offices, or as presidents of diocesan school boards, Directors of Catholic Charities, and of other diocesan committees. They are gradually approaching equal occupational status with the clergy, an historic advance from their traditional position of subservience in the Church structure.

Endnotes

1. Jean Danielou, *The Ministry of Women in the Early Church,* London, Faith Press, 1961, p. 7.

2. Ursula King, *Women and Spirituality,* London, Macmillan, 1989, p. 24.

3. Leonard Swidler, *Biblical Affirmations of Women,* Philadelphia, Westminster, 1979. See also his article, "Jesus was a Feminist," *Catholic World,* January, 1971, pp. 177-183.

4. E. Jane Via, "Women in the Gospel of Luke," pp. 38-55, in Ursula King, ed., *Women in the World's Religions,* New York Paragon, 1987.

5. "Women in the Church," *Origins,* vol. 9, December 27, 1979, pp. 450-454 (Task Force Report of Catholic Biblical Association).

6. Mary Lawrence McKenna, *Women in the Church,* New York, Kenedy, 1967, p. 40.

7. *Ibid.,* p. 53.

8. *Ibid.,* p. 51.

9. *Ibid.*, p. 96.

10. *Ibid.*, p. 96.

11. *Ibid.*, p. 97.

12. Elizabeth Clark and Herbert Richardson, *Women and Religion*, New York, Harper & Row, 1977, p. 7.

13. McKenna, *op. cit.*, p. 97.

14. G. Saint-Laurent, "St. Ambrose's Theology of the Consecrated Virgin," *Review for Religious*, vol. 41, no. 3, 1982, pp. 358-359.

15. Diane C. Desautels, "An Early Christian Rite Revised: Consecrated Virgins Living in the World," *Review for Religious*, vol. 49, no. 4, 1990, pp. 567-580.

16. Georges H. Tavard, *Woman in Christian Tradition*, University of Notre Dame Press, 1973, p. 92.

17. See Jerome, Letter 22, "To Eustochium: The Virgin's Profession," *Select Letters of St. Jerome*, Cambridge, Harvard University Press, 1933.

18. Aime Georges Martimort, *Deaconesses, An Historical Study*, San Francisco, Ignatius Press, 1986, p. 242.

19. Jean Danielou and Henri Marrou, *The First Six Hundred Years*, New York, Paulist Press, 1979, p. 164.

20. *Ibid.*, p. 240.

21. McKenna, *op. cit.*, p. 86.

22. Martimort, *op. cit.*, pp. 245-246.

23. Danielou, *op. cit.*, p. 7.

24. *Ibid.*, p. 22.

25. Joan Morris, *The Lady Was a Bishop*, New York, Macmillan, 1973, p. 17.

26. Kenedy's *Catholic Directory*, for 1990, lists 106 abbots but no abbesses. Belmont Abbey in North Carolina was, until 1982, the only one with territorial jurisdiction.

27. Morris, *op. cit.*, p.73.

28. See Elizabeth Clark and Herbert Richardson, *op. cit.*, chapter 6, "Jerome, The Exaltation of Christian Virginity."

29. Mary Ann Donovan, *Sisterhood as Power*, New York, Crossroad, 1989, p. 14.

30. See Lena Eckenstein, *Women Under Monasticism*, New (York, Russel and Russel, 1963, chap. 10.

31. Joseph H. Fichter, *A Sociologist Looks at Religion*, chap. 10, "Catholic Sisterhoods: Tradition and Modernity," Wilmington, Michael Glazier, 1988.

32. M. P. Trauth, "Mary Ward," *New Catholic Encyclopedia*, vol. 14, 1957, pp. 808-809. Because she was considered "rebellious," Mary Ward was imprisoned in a Munich convent for a short time. In 1909 Pius X reinstated her posthumously as foundress of the Institute.

33. Leon Cardinal Suenens, *The Nun in the World: Religious and the Apostolate*, Westminster, Newman Press, 1963, p. 36.

34. "On Educating Youth," *The Catholic Mind*, June, 1952, vol. 50, pp. 376-380.

35. The Pope's letter and the Vatican document are published in *Origins*, vol. 13, July 7, 1983, pp. 129-142.

36. Dorothy Vidulich, "Finding a Founder," pp. 161-171, in Ann Patrick Ware, ed., *Mid-Wives of the Future: American Sisters Tell Their Story*, Kansas City, Leaven Press, 1985.

37. Ann Ware, *op. cit.*, p. 1.

Chapter Three

Holy Father Church

The description of the Roman Catholic Church, as though it were fixed in the female gender, seems to have been a long tradition acceptable even at high ecclesiastical levels. No less an authority than the Second Vatican Council can be quoted in this regard. In his opening speech to the Council, Pope John's first words were: "Mother Church rejoices that, by the singular gift of Divine Providence, the longed-for day has finally dawned." The first document issued by the Council in 1963, *Lumen Gentium,* is the dogmatic constitution on the Church, to which it applies the female pronoun throughout. "In *her* relationship with Christ, the Church is a kind of sacrament, or sign of intimate union with God, and of the unity of all mankind. *She* is also an instrument for the achievement of such union and unity." (art. 1) The Church is unabashedly called a woman, a bride, a wife. "Having become the model of a man loving his wife as his own body, Christ loves the Church as His bride. For *her* part, the Church is subject to *her* head." (art. 7)

The analogy of the Church as wife and bride of Christ is as old as Paul's letter to the Ephesians, where he counsels, "Husbands, love your wives in the same way that Christ loved the Church and gave His life for *her*." (Eph. 5:25) St. Paul's analogy has now lost popularity with Catholic feminists who dislike his advice to submit themselves to their husband's authority. "For a husband has authority over his wife in the same way Christ has authority over the Church." (Eph. 5:22) No devout Catholic seriously objects to the fact that the Church should be submissive to Christ and that all Christians should be obedient to His teachings.

Catholics commonly talk about "Holy Mother Church," a title highlighted by the Council's frequent references to her maternal role. "She brings forth, to a new and immortal life, children who are conceived of the Holy Spirit and born of God." But the Church also remains a virgin and "preserves with virginal purity an integral faith, a firm hope, and a sincere charity." (*Lumen Gentium,* art. 64) Then also, "the Church community exercises a true motherhood toward souls who are to be led to Christ." (*Presbyterorum Ordinis,* art. 6) The bishops are advised that in propounding Catholic doctrine they "should manifest the Church's maternal solicitude for all men, believers or not." (*Christus Dominus,* art. 13)

Female Religiosity

Constantly over the centuries, females—more than males—have shown deep filial devotion to Mother Church. Every survey that attempts to measure gender differences in religiosity finds that females are "holier" than males. They attend religious services more frequently, pray more often, hold firmer beliefs, cooperate more in Church programs. This is true at all age levels, from childhood to senior citizen, of both single and married women, of working women and homemakers. It was true of Catholics before the Second Vatican Council, as well as of more recent studies.[1] Although no instrument of social science can measure their internal sanctity, their holiness in the "sight of God," we may assume that they surpass males also in this respect.

Years ago, before we knew anything about *aggiornamento,* I published an article in *Integrity,* in which I sought "explanations" why piety seemed to be more a female than a male attribute.[2] I naively concluded that God does not create holier souls for female bodies than for male bodies. I questioned that women are instinctively more emotional than men, or even that emotionality is a usable criterion for the measurement of religiosity. The only credible interpretation seemed to be that cultural expectations differ across gender lines. This means that the religious behavior of the individual male or female tends to conform to the behavioral patterns of each sex that are current in the contemporary culture.[3]

Unfortunately, in the American culture and in Western society generally, there is implied in these expectations a kind of double standard of religious behavior. The little girl is trained to be more pious than the little boy; she is supposed to behave better in church and to go there more often. Teenage girls are more likely than boys to participate in parish clubs, Bible study, religious discussion groups, and church choirs. It is considered the "normal thing" that adult women outnumber men at church services, receiving Holy Communion, directing CCD programs, and joining the parents' club of the parish. Religious Sisters outnumber priests and brothers by almost three to one. Is it any wonder that religion and church are often thought of as feminine prerogatives?

The religious strength of Catholic wives and mothers was boldly proclaimed early in the century by Leonora Barry Lake, who was an organizer for the Catholic Total Abstinence Union. She demonstrated that women are the guardians of religion: "Who have built the churches? If you answer truly, you must say 'the women.' Who makes the man go to Mass on Sunday morning? Who sends the children to Sunday School? The woman."[4] She was a feminist ahead of her time and wanted women to use their religious strength and spiritual influence in the promotion of social change as well as in the preservation of family morality.

Yet, organized Christianity is dominated by males, and this is even more the case in Judaism. We know that holiness, religiosity, piety—all the virtues in which women excel men—are the very qualities expected of seminarians, deacons, priests, and bishops. If vocation recruiters are really seeking the best qualified persons to train for the sacred functions of religion, they should not completely ignore girls as candidates for the seminary. In the Catholic Church, the blunt answer is that an historical pattern of exclusion, conforming to the Jewish culture of the Apostolic Age, has been continued into this American century. Long-embedded social habits and mores are hard to break or replace. People tend to think of them as though they were natural, logical, God-given, and immutable.

When religious Sisters began to raise their voices after the Council, the question was asked: "If woman is more religious than man, why is man (even young boys) more appropriate to worship ceremonies; why must women enter the sanctuary as an intruder? How explain the fact that the Church (and churches) have so few women visible in official roles?" Ethne Kennedy, chair person of the National Assembly of Women Religious, pointed to the large numbers of women in church services: "Considering the investment of women in the working church, one wonders how church officials can realistically question whether or not society is ready for women in pastoral ministry. Would not a more reasonable response be, 'how can we prepare society for full participation of women in every area and on every level?' A gloomy reflection might even be: 'How much longer will women tolerate such oppression in the community of Jesus Christ?'"[5]

It can probably be said without much dispute that the Church as a cultural institution imitates the patterns of male-female relations current in the larger society. The comparison has often been made that Jesus and his disciples simply accepted the typical Jewish customs concerning women. John Paul II repudiates this allegation: "In all of Jesus' teaching, as well as in His behavior, one can find nothing which reflects the discrimination against women prevalent in His day." This means to say that, "Jesus' attitude to the women whom He meets in the course of His Messianic service reflects the eternal plan of God, who, in creating each one of them, chooses her and loves her in Christ."[6] This interpretation helps us to understand the attitude of Christ toward women, but the historical explanation has to be that Christians in His time, and in ours, have never really imitated Christ.

Prejudicial attitudes tend to permeate the whole culture and make no exception for gender. In other words, many women seem satisfied with their status in the Church. Socially-aware nuns complain about their lack of self-determination, but one of the earliest surveys found that Catholic males were more favorable than females to ecclesiastical opportunities for women. Sally Cunneen reported in 1968 that the majority of her respondents—but more males than females—thought that women should be lectors and commentators at the public liturgy. The same comparison occurred on the question whether women should be ordained deaconesses. In subsequent surveys, the crucial matter of women's ordination to the priesthood barely found a majority in favor; but even here, women still gave less support than men.[7]

Sisters' Liberation

When Betty Friedan gathered a group of women at Milwaukee in 1966, to establish the National Organization for Women, she counted two Catholic nuns among the dedicated feminists. By this time, it was more than two decades since the religious Sisters had begun their move toward modernization. As early as 1941 the search for higher academic degrees was sparked by Sr. Bertrande Meyers' book on *The Education of Sisters.* Consciousness-raising had been increased among the women religious in the Sisters Formation Conference, begun in 1954, which expanded further educational opportunities for them. In the practical realm of work and life these cultural changes had already been embraced by the Maryknoll Sisters, who developed "a life-style that supported their ministry without the encumbrance of obsolete customs from other times and places." In other words, the much advertised women's liberation movement was already anticipated by congregations of religious who were thought to be the least liberated women in America.

Every Catholic knows that religious Sisters had been piously submissive over the generations, obedient not only to the Holy See through their religious vows, but also subservient to their bishop and to the local pastor in whose parish school they taught. "Many sisters," wrote Angelica Seng, "have been conditioned, in the name of a pseudo-reverence and obedience, to regard their relations with priests, and especially with the pastor, as one of silence, obedience and dependence. Perhaps it is something akin to a father-daughter relationship, in which the daughter never reaches the adolescent age."[8] This description was no longer accurate, even when it was presented just after the Council. By that time, the American Sisterhoods had moved into self-conscious adulthood.

The American Sisterhoods had already been under way to the *aggiornamento* when Pope Pius XII called the major superiors of religious congregations to Rome for international conferences in 1950 and again in 1952. He suggested that they update the professional training of the Sisters. The American Sisters moved faster than the Pope expected, and are said to have been the inspiration for Cardinal Suenens' influential book about the *Nun in the World*. In the spirit of collegiality, the Conference of Major Superiors of Women (CMSW) changed its name to the Leadership Conference of Women Religious, whose president, Sister Theresa Kane, confronted the Pope at his public appearance in Washington. Meanwhile, other groups organized across congregational lines, like the National Assembly of Women Religious, the National Coalition of American Nuns, the Network for Social Justice. At Woodstock, in 1969, to everyone's surprise, the Association of Contemplative Sisters organized, and were seen as a "clear act of defiant self-determination."[9] It had already been said that, "when John XXIII convoked the Second Vatican Council, many Sisters were ready for it." In comparative retrospect, it could well be argued that "few groups in the church responded to the decrees of the Second Vatican Council, with the alacrity shown by American Sisters."[10]

The Sisterhoods took seriously the mandate of the Holy Father, that they conscientiously study their own history and constitutions and then make revisions needed to modernize their life and ministry. They sometimes aroused the patriarchal ideology of their local Ordinary. Some members of the hierarchy were "angry and indignant over decisions made by Sisterhoods within their dioceses, and were determined to do something about it." Bishops in the Catholic Church have the patriarchal power to force changes and to reverse them.

"This happened in 1965, when Archbishop Karl Alter legislated for the lives of the Glenmary Sisters and caused half of them to leave their community and form a lay group. It occurred again in 1968, when 400 of the 450 Sisters of the Immaculate Heart of Mary chose the same alternative rather than allow Cardinal McIntyre to overrule their chapter decisions." Episcopal interference of this kind was permitted by the Vatican, even though it contravened the philosophy of responsibility and initiative that the Council had encouraged. Such interference by the local hierarchy caused pain and confusion among the Sisters, who could rightly complain with Mother Austin Carroll: "We have done all that Rome has asked of us. If we were misled when we followed the bishops' directives before, how can we be certain that we are not being misguided now?"[11]

One of the remarkable changes among the American Sisters in the decade before the Second Vatican Council was their sharp rise in academic achievements. Increasing numbers followed the papal advice that they be trained to compete with their professional peers. Many of them got to "know the world" at a level perhaps higher than most Catholic lay women. It appears that some of them were now "too smart" to put up with patriarchal discrimination and episcopal whims. In her study of Sisters who left the convent, Helen Ebaugh tested the hypothesis that, "Orders with higher levels of education lost more members than orders with lower levels of education."[12]

Many of the nuns who left the convent opted for marriage, and some of them married resigned priests; but this does not mean that they left the Church or lost interest in the works of ministry. Many who left the convent felt that they did not belong there in the sense that they had no religious vocation; some were dissatisfied with community life and felt that they lacked "personal fulfillment." Sister Augusta Neal concludes that, "the over-all trends in numbers leaving are more social than psychic, caused by concomitant trends in the conditions of the society and the Church's response to them."[13]

The Sexist Hierarchy

The tendency among the obedient Catholic laity was always to mold their social and cultural attitudes according to the teaching of the bishops. There were, of course, some exceptions to this pattern, even in the old days before the Second Vatican Council. The historical evidence is clear, however, that most of the hierarchy were opposed to women suffrage, child labor laws, women's higher education, women working outside the home, and the Equal Rights Amendment. Catholic pressure groups against women's liberation included lay women themselves in organizations like the Catholic Daughters of America, Daughters of Isabella, National Council of Catholic Women, and the International Federation of Catholic Alumnae.

The strongest opponent of women's liberation, who was in his day the most prominent Catholic in America, was James Cardinal Gibbons. In 1904 he preached that, "Woman does not today exercise the right of suffrage. She cannot vote, and I am heartily glad of it. I hope the day will never come when she can vote, and if the right is granted her, I hope she will regret it." At the First National Anti-Suffrage Convention in 1916, he sent a message of approval and support. He "maintained that he spoke for the dignity of women and asserted that feminists would rob women of character and substitute masculine boldness for feminine honor and character."[14] Boston's Cardinal William O'Connell also opposed women's suffrage, as well as child labor laws and the Equal Rights Amendment.

The Bishops' Program of Social Reconstruction of 1919 was an admirable and prophetic document. It grudgingly conceded the right to vote and also demanded equal pay for women, but the bishops still wanted women to stay home from work. They encouraged employers to hire men instead of women.[15] Even the famous social apostle, Monsignor John A. Ryan, as spokesman for the NCWC, felt that women already had workers' protection under the law and did not require a further Equal Rights Amendment. After American women won the right to vote in the Nineteenth Constitutional Amendment in 1921, the bishops turned their wrath against the women's Equal Rights Amendment. Having lost the fight against women's suffrage, the hierarchy tried to hold the line against further and "radical" demands.

The Amendment, which the bishops thought dangerous to women and harmful of family morality, simply said that, "Equality of rights under the law shall not be denied or abridged by the United States or any State on the basis of sex. Congress and the several States shall have power, within their respective jurisdiction, to enforce this article by appropriate legislation." With the civil rights movement of the 1960's, the bill was resurrected and then sent to the States for ratification in 1972. Catholic organizations rallied in opposition: The NCCW organized a massive letter-writing campaign to State legislators; the Knights of Columbus, Holy Name Society, and Catholic Daughters passed resolutions against it. The bishops themselves, in 1972 and again in 1975, were fearful of the "doctrinaire character and broad sweep" of the Amendment.

When it looked as though the Amendment would gain ratification by the States, some of the bishops had a change of heart. In 1982 a joint statement was issued by a number of bishops who called upon the legislatures to ratify the Equal Rights Amendment. Among the signatories were several archbishops who were sometimes known as "liberals:" James Casey of Denver, Raymond Hunthausen of Seattle, Rembert Weakland of Milwaukee.[16] Their intervention came too late, because the Amendment failed of the necessary votes for ratification. Oddly enough, it was a Catholic woman, Phyllis Schlafly, who was the most aggressive opponent of the movement for women's rights.

The institutional and collective beginning of the bishops' concern for the "woman problem" appeared in the 1971 document of the Bishops' Synod, *Justitia in Mundo*, which urged that, "women should have their own share of responsibility and participation in the community life of society and likewise of the Church." In the following year, the bishops formed an Ad Hoc Committee on the "Role of Women in Society and the Church." Nothing happens quickly at the hierarchical level. Five years later, in 1977, the bishops conducted a survey concerning the church roles of women. In 1983, Pope John Paul wrote to the bishops, promoting dialogue with religious women. It then took about four years (from 1984 to 1988) to produce the first "Pastoral Response to Womens' Concerns for Church and Society."[17]

The bishops condemn sexism as a "heinous" sin. They write that, "sexism, directly opposed to Christian humanism and feminism, is the erroneous belief, or conviction, or attitude, that one sex, female or male, is superior to the other in the very order of creation, or by the very nature of things. When anyone believes that men are inherently superior to women, or that women are inherently superior to men, then he or she is guilty of sexism."[18] Women tend to see sexism as a male sin expressed in misogyny and resulting in patriarchy. "Sexism pervades structures and organizations, individuals and communities."[19]

The American Bishops also condemn clericalism which shows a patronizing and demeaning attitude toward women. While full equal status has not been achieved, women may cooperate in governance of the Church, serve as judges on the tribunal, may become the chancellor of a diocese. While the diaconal ordination is still denied to them, women may "participate in all liturgical ministries that do not require ordination." The bishops recommend "the inclusion of women as consultors and members of bishops' committees, as administrators and participants in diocesan and universal synods, as collaborators in decision-making and policy-setting processes."[20]

Patriarchy

Not all Catholic feminists are satisfied that the American Bishops have now caught up with gender equality. Indeed, many complain that the bishops are still patronizing the women and cannot take credit for church equality until all positions are open to women. They argue further that the bishops should focus their attention on the problem of men. The solution for women's inequality cannot be reached until the male, patriarchal cause of that equality has been remedied. Schussler-Fiorenza complains that "scant attention has been paid to the patriarchalization of Christian ministry and church." Among the early Christians there was an "insistence on the religious equality of believers as sisters and brothers" but also a "hierarchically ordered superiority of ministers."[21]

The most bitter American attack on ecclesial misogyny came from Mary Daly, who has now fully abandoned Christianity and Catholicism. I first knew her as a brilliant and hopeful young theologian who performed as guest speaker in the seminar I conducted at Harvard University on the subject of "Women and Religion." At that time, she could still say that, "events have moved rapidly in ten years; we are now living in an age characterized by a heightened sense of hope and of personal responsibility."[22] The guarded optimism she expressed to my seminar students turned to disappointment and despair. In the 1975 edition of her work, *The Church and the Second Sex*, she wrote a new Introduction and labeled it, "Feminist Post-Christian." Ten years later she declared her complete repudiation of Christianity.

The focus of Daly's continuing anger and resentment of Christianity, and specifically Catholicism, is the patriarchal character of the Church and its theology: "If God is male, male is God," is the slogan that leads her to the most virulent anti-male philosophy. Her second book, *Beyond God, the Father*, is an all-out attack on the patriarchy of the Church and also definitely alienates her from the whole Christian tradition.[23] Having left not only the Roman Church but all forms of religious expression of a male deity, she has dedicated herself to the empowerment of feminism in its most radical form.[24] In spite of this estrangement from her former associates, she has probably "contributed greatly to the consciousness-raising of women within the Church."[25]

With the agitation about reducing the impact of patriarchy in the Church, there naturally grew an awareness that Christian prayers and liturgies are couched in the language of patriarchy. Just as people said *she* or *her* in talking of the Church, so they tend to say *He* and *Him* in reference to God. Feminists became increasingly annoyed that the language of prayer and liturgy is predominantly masculine, beginning with God the Father and God the Son. There was then a demand to introduce a "genderless language" which would pray in the name of the Creator, and of the Redeemer and the Sanctifier. The insistence on "inclusive language" meant that hymns had to be revised and prayer books reprinted. The sexist language of Rite Four, in the Canon of the Mass, is easily changed to alternative pronouns and is most frequently used in feminist liturgies.

The problem of sexist language is a detail that does not escape the American Bishops in their 1988 Pastoral Response. "On every level of communication," they write, "we recommend avoiding language that is insensitive to women. Especially in liturgical, and educational settings, we should use language that expresses inclusivity wherever appropriate and permissible. Customs and practices that do not promote the equal dignity of women must be adjusted to reflect more faithfully the essential teachings and traditions of the Church." (229) More specifically in their 1990 meeting, the bishops declared that "words such as *men, sons, brothers, brethren, forefathers, fraternity, and brotherhood,* which were once understood as inclusive generic terms, today are often understood as referring only to males." Therefore, these terms should not be used when the reference is meant to be generic.[26]

Women who criticize the bishops for centering their attention on the "woman problem" argue that men are the problem, that male attitudes of superiority and practices that are discriminatory must be reformed before all else. The bishops do take notice of this fact when they say that the problems women face in the church and in the society cannot be remedied in full until men reform their habits. This is directed to husbands and fathers in family life, to male employers everywhere, including those in the church, and to the clergy themselves in their ongoing dialogue with women. "We challenge men to become involved in changing the structures and patterns of social and ecclesial life that account for the persistent oppression of women." (230)

As though to make amends for the centuries of patriarchal oppression, the bishops actually recommend "the theological preparation of women to preach the Gospel and to use their gifts as preachers in the church, in retreats, and other spiritual conferences." (221) Women may also be helpful in that ultimate masculine bastion, the seminary. "We further recommend that women be included on the faculties and staffs of institutions responsible for the formation and education of candidates for the diaconate and priesthood." (228)

The Ultimate Equality

The distance that American Catholic women have gone on the way to gender emancipation may be measured in comparison with the first best-seller of a century ago. The author asserted that woman is "by nature the more spiritual of the two sexes, being prone to all that is most heroic, and endowed by the Creator with unlimited power for good or for evil. Mothers were living images of God in their unsleeping watchfulness and unfathomable tenderness. The home was woman's God-appointed sphere, a place where true woman held sway, a place where woman could be a queen and become a saint."[27] Eighty years later, in 1971, the Synod of Bishops changed all that and suggested that women need no longer be confined to home and family. "We also urge that women should have their own share of responsibility and participation in the community life of society and likewise of the Church." (*Justitia in Mundo*, par. 42)

In his evaluation of the 1971 Synod of Bishops, Schillebeeckx remarks that, "at present, the discontent in the Church is fiercest among women. Moreover, it is no longer just discontent as a result of the negative experiences of women with the institutionalized churches but a very conscious accusation. Above all, in North America this discontent is organized into a deliberate 'Women's Church' movement which intentionally accuses the patriarchal, masculine character of the Church and its leaders, as indeed of society."[28] The Women's Church Movement, the *ekklesia* of women, is bonded by a "feminist Christian spirituality," and includes all categories of women's liberation: the Sisterhoods, the laywomen in ministry, the wives of deacons, the wives of priests. "It rejects the idolatrous worship of maleness and articulates the divine image in female human existence and language."[29]

The demand for equality between the sexes is a demand for justice. Essentially, this means that the rights of women must be protected with the same vigor that is expended on the rights of men. Whatever benefits and opportunities accrue to males must also be extended to females. In the economic institution this translates into equal pay and promotional opportunities. In the realm of politics it means equal treatment before the law as well as appointment, or election, to all positions of authority. Analogously, this should mean that the ecclesiastical institution should provide the same opportunities for women as for men.

We are told by the American Bishops that all ministries, all church tasks and positions, are open to women candidates, except those which require a minister in holy orders. This concession almost matches the proposal of Archbishop Paul Hallinan, at the Second Vatican Council, who complained that the Church has been slow in claiming for women the right of suffrage and economic equality. He proposed that the liturgical functions of lector and acolyte, as well as the Office of Deaconess, be opened to women.[30] By this time, St. Joan's Alliance had been fighting more than a half century for women's equality in the Church. It began as a Catholic suffrage movement in London in 1911 and developed into an international network, insisting on women's admission to priestly ordination.

The demand for equal rights in the Church is a demand in the virtue of justice, which may challenge the fact that the occupational structure of ecclesiastical authority is exclusively in the hands of ordained males. As the hierarchy is presently constituted, it is patriarchal at all levels of administration. While women may claim equal rights for "job opportunities" in the Church, they are not allowed to claim rights to the entrance requirement for these jobs: sacramental ordination.

The legalistic response to the demand of justice as an entry to ordination is that the grace of vocation is a free gift of God, to which no one can claim a right in justice. The privilege of a priestly vocation can be actualized only when it is recognized and accepted by a bishop who administers the sacrament of holy orders. This does not mean, as is sometimes alleged, that a female is inherently non-ordainable. While the Holy See continues to deny that holy orders are permissible for women, the Bishops of the Episcopal Church have conferred valid holy orders on women candidates.[31] We have no way of knowing whether God calls Catholic women to the priesthood and we have no way of disproving the priestly vocation claimed by the women who attended the Detroit Ordination Conference in November, 1975.[32]

Aside from claiming ordination as a right for women, another argument asserts that it is a necessity for the eucharistic needs of the Catholic community. In 1958, I addressed the Annual Convention of Vocation Directors in Milwaukee and suggested a quick end to the priest shortage. I said that the number of vocations to the priesthood probably would be doubled, if girls were admitted to the seminary. The suggestion was greeted with loud and prolonged laughter. The very idea was so ridiculous that a news reporter asked me later whether I had really said it, and whether I objected to it being printed in his paper. On another occasion, in a Symposium at Boston College, Father Richard McBrien was asked whether his seminary would accept a woman candidate for the priesthood. He taught then at a National Seminary for Delayed Vocations, and the lady who asked the question, a college professor, was certainly in the midst of a "delayed" vocation. His answer also drew a laugh. He said his seminary would accept the lady if she could find a bishop willing to incardinate her into his diocese.

The Women's Ordination Conference follows the lead of St. Joan's Alliance in challenging the notion that women priests are unthinkable in the Catholic Church. An increasing number of Catholic women have completed theological and biblical studies, sometimes surpassing the academic standards required for the ordination of males. The bishops themselves said, "we encourage dioceses to provide more scholarships for the theological, ministerial, religious, and spiritual education of qualified women, so they may better serve the Church in the fields of teaching, administration, counseling, and direction."[33] If these women feel they have a vocation to the priesthood, however, their only obstacle is their sex. Several of my former students have switched to Lutheran or Episcopal divinity schools, with the intention of seeking ordination there.

The ultimate equality for women in the Catholic Church opens the whole occupational structure for them from top to bottom. They move from girl acolytes to seminary students, through the transitional diaconate to the priesthood. Then, they should be appointed, selected and promoted according to the same criteria employed for male priests. In their parochial ministry they may receive monsignoral honors, if deserved, become vicar-generals, if competent, earning elevation to the bishopric, the College of Cardinals, even to the papacy. Sex discrimination should go the way of ethnic and racial discrimination. In the course I teach on Women and Religion, I conclude my final lecture of the semester with the statement: "We shall witness the complete removal of discrimination in the Catholic Church on the day when there is a pregnant Pope who is either African or Asian."

Endnotes

1. See Joseph H. Fichter, *Social Relations in the Urban Parish,* Chicago, University of Chicago Press, 1954, p. 91. In all religious groups, "it is clear that women had more othodox attitudes and more traditional behavior than men." Dean Hoge, *Commitment on Campus*, Philadelphia, Westminster, 1974, p. 110.

2. "Why Aren't Males So Holy?" *Integrity*, May, 1955, pp. 3-11.

3. Emphasis has recently been returned to innate psychological explanations. See Carol Gilligan, *In A Different Voice*, Cambridge, Harvard University Press, 1982.

4. Quoted by Debra Campbell, "Reformers and Activists," pp. 152-181, in Karen Kennelly, *op. cit.*

5. Ethne Kennedy, "The Changing World of Women," pp. 9-18, in *Women in Ministry*, Chicago, NAWR, 1972.

6. John Paul II, Apostolic Letter, *Mulieris Dignitatem*, August 15, 1988, Washington, U. S. Catholic Conference, pp. 52f.

7. Sally Cunneen, *Sex: Female; Religion: Catholic*, New York, Holt, Rinehart and Winston, 1968, chapter 9, "Church Roles for Women."

8. M. Angelica Seng, "The Sister in the New City," pp. 229-262, in M. Charles Borromeo Muckenhirn, ed., *The Changing Sister*, Notre Dame, Fides, 1965.

9. Mary Jo Weaver, *New Catholic Women*, San Francisco, Harper & Row, 1985, p. 104.

10. Mary Ewens, "Women in the Convent," pp. 17-47, in Karen Kennelly, ed., *American Catholic Women*, New York, Macmillan, 1989.

11. *Ibid.*, p. 43.

12. Helen Rose Ebaugh, *Out of the Cloister*, Austin, University of Texas Press, 1977, p. 55.

13. Marie Augusta Neal, *Catholic Sisters in Transition*, Wilmington, Glazier, 1984, p. 23.

14. Quoted by James Kennelly, "A Question of Equality," pp. 125-151, in Karen Kennelly, ed., *American Catholic Women*, New York, Macmillan, 1989.

15. *Ibid.*, p. 140.

16. See the *National Catholic Reporter*, June 18, 1982. See also, "The U. S. Bishops and the ERA," *Origins*, January 3, 1985.

17. For the various accounts of developments, see *Origins*, July 7, 1982, March 21 and October 3, 1985, April 21, 1988.

18. Bishops Victor Blake and Raymond Lucker, "Male and Female God Created Them," *Origins*, November 5, 1981.

19. Mary E. Hunt, "Roman Catholic Ministry: Patriarchal Past: Feminist Future," pp. 31-42, in Maureen Dwyer, *New Woman, New Church, New Ministry*, Baltimore, 1978, Proceedings of Second Conference on the Ordination of Roman Catholic Women.

20. "Partners in the Mystery of Redemption," 218-226. See also, Ruth Wallace, "Catholic Women and the Creation of New Social Reality," *Gender and Society,* March, 1988, pp. 24-38.

21. Elisabeth Schussler-Fiorenza, *In Memory of Her,* New York, Crossroad, 1983, p. 285.

22. Mary Daly, *The Church and the Second Sex,* New York, Harper & Row, 1968, p. 9.

23. Mary Daly, *Beyond God the Father: Toward a Philosophy of Women's Liberation,* Boston, Beacon Press, 1985.

24. Mary Daly, *Gyn/Ecology,* Boston, Beacon Press, 1978; and *Pure Lust,* Boston, Beacon Press, 1984.

25. Rosemary Rader, "Catholic Feminism: Its Impact on U. S. Catholic Women," pp. 182-197, in Karen Kennelly, ed., *op. cit.*

26. "Inclusive Language in Liturgy: Scriptural Texts," *Origins,* November 29, 1990, pp. 405-408.

27. Bernard O'Reilly, *Mirror of True Womanhood,* New York, 1892, paraphrased by Karen Kennelly, "Ideals of American Catholic Womanhood," *op. cit.,* p. 3.

28. Schillebeeckx, *op. cit.,* p. 236.

29. Schussler-Fiorenza, *op. cit.,* p. 346. See especially, Rosemary Ruether, *Women-Church: Theology and Practice,* San Francisco, Harper & Row, 1985.

30. See Vincent Yzermans, ed., *American Participation in the Vatican Council,* New York, 1967, p. 202.

31. The *Apostolicae Curae* on Anglican holy orders has been subject to much controversy. See Francis Clark, *Anglican Orders and Defect of Intention,* 1956.

32. Described by Fran Ferder, *Called to Break Bread,* Mt. Ranier, Quixote Center, 1978.

33. "Partners in the Mystery of Redemption," par. 226.

Chapter Four

Optional Marriage

Many articles have been published and endless discussions conducted, under the title of "Optional Celibacy," for the priests of the Roman Catholic Church; but the fact is that the Church does not allow any option, or choice, in this matter. Furthermore, what has happened among the resigned priests is that they have taken the option for marriage. Of course, they had freely chosen to become priests, but in doing so they automatically had to accept a permanent celibate state of life. When they seek a dispensation to allow marriage—which is now seldom and reluctantly granted—they are told that they must relinquish the priesthood.

Everyone knows that the option exists for the priests of the Eastern Uniate rite either to marry or to remain single, but only before ordination. In discussing the life and ministry of Latin-rite clergy, the Fathers of the Second Vatican Council were careful to point out that celibacy is "not indeed, demanded by the nature of the priesthood, as is evident from the practice of the primitive Church and from the tradition of the Eastern churches. In these churches, in addition to all bishops and those others who by a gift of grace choose to observe celibacy, there also exist married priests of outstanding merit." (*Presbyterorum Ordinis*, art. 16)

This solemn recognition of virtuous married priests in the non-Latin rites, and of those others who *chose* to remain unmarried, did not soften the Council's adamant objection to married clergy in the West. They went on to say in another document that "total continence embraced on behalf of the Kingdom of Heaven has always been held in particular honor by the Church as being a sign of charity and a stimulus toward it, as well as a unique fountain of spiritual fertility in the world." (*Lumen Gentium*, art. 42) While the Council was still in session, Michael Novak speculated that "there seemed to be an almost absolute block in the minds of some of the bishops against uniting marriage to holy orders. It seemed to outsiders that the celibacy of these bishops had been so precarious, at least unconsciously, that if they had had the choice, they would never have accepted us."[1]

Clergy Opinions

The prelates who assembled at the Second Vatican Council were at a broad hierarchical distance from the priests who were ministering to Catholics at the parish level. We could be sure also that their opinions about clergy celibacy and marriage would be at a different level from that of the Council Fathers. In a pre-Council research study I had noted that the law of celibacy had become an obstacle to the recruitment of seminarians and to the retention of priests. But there was much uncertainty about the extent to which the American clergy were genuinely concerned about the "forbidden topic," which had supposedly become "non-debatable" at the Council.

In the year following the close of the Council, I undertook to open the question again to a national sample of diocesan priests. "During the past year," I asked, "have you discussed this question with your fellow diocesan priests?" A large majority (86%) of the responding priests said they had "frequently," or "occasionally," talked among themselves about optional celibacy. On a further question, six out of ten (62%) voted in favor of freedom of choice for priests to marry. Almost two-thirds (64%) agreed that it should be possible to have voluntary resignation, or an "honorable discharge," from the priesthood. An opinion more pertinent to the current discussions among the CORPUS membership was that the overwhelming majority (93%) agreed that the married resigned priests should be allowed to return to the sacraments and remain married.[2]

These statistical findings are now commonplace, even old-fashioned, but they were a bold revelation twenty-five years ago, when a research project on this topic had to be almost surreptitious. The proposal to do this research was instituted by a cautious St. Louis priest who wanted to be anonymous. He asked Robert Hoyt, editor of the *National Catholic Reporter*, to promote a survey of priests' attitudes about clergy celibacy. This unnamed priest, together with a group of fellow clergy, felt a need for caution because they did not want to get in trouble with their bishop. The spokesman for this anonymous group later revealed himself to be Father Frank Matthews, a pastor in the St. Louis Archdiocese, and Director of the Catholic Radio and Television Apostolate.

Hoyt agreed to make a financial contribution to the research for the right of first publication of the results. The St. Louis priest group provided the remaining funds and contracted with me to conduct the research program.[3] From the beginning they were eager that the American Bishops "find out what the priests are thinking," especially in the matter of optional marriage. They wanted the results channeled to the American hierarchy and through them to the Vatican and to the Pope himself. They were sure that certain progressive bishops—Steven Leven of San Antonio; Ernest Primeau of Manchester; James Shannon of St. Paul—would be willing to "make a case" with the hierarchy and act as an intermediary committee in presenting the research findings to church officials at Rome.[4]

Probably the best advice Bishop Shannon gave us was that the research findings should not be a secret and confidential report reserved to the hierarchy and the Vatican. The whole Church community should be informed. Since the questionnaire reached into every diocese in the country, there was neither need nor effort to keep the study confidential. Many priests said the study sparked debates among their colleagues. Others asked to be included in the survey. Only one man refused to respond, and it was because the questionnaire "does not say that the survey has the approval of the bishop." Inevitably, word of the research project spread among the American hierarchy, several of whom complained to the Cardinal Secretary of

State at the Vatican, so that "the matter was brought to the attention of the Holy See."

In December, 1966, I mailed the statistical report of the survey to all the Bishop Ordinaries in the United States and, at the same time, released it for publication in the *National Catholic Reporter*. By this time, the Apostolic Delegate in Washington, Archbishop Egidio Vagnozzi, had been alerted to the survey. He wrote to me: "I have been asked to recommend to you that in your prudence you not publish the data of this investigation without first bringing the matter to the attention of the National Conference of Catholic Bishops and the appropriate Congregation of the Holy See." His request that I "use prudence" came too late and he did not appreciate the publicity that was later given to the "Fichter Report." He publicly denounced me for sending the questionnaire to the "wrong" priests. He said that "the group was composed of older priests who had not been promoted—possibly for good reason—and of young, rather immature clerics."[5]

Only a few of the bishops acknowledged receipt of the preliminary report of research findings. What seemed to irritate some of these hierarchs and to arouse national attention to the survey report was the "sensationalism" of the revelation that many priests approved the option to marry. This "fearful" topic that had been banned from the floor of debate at the Council was now wide open to common discussion and debate. A subsequent survey, financed by the bishops themselves, also found that the clergy "tend to support a change in the celibacy regulations."[6]

It is a peculiar historical coincidence that I conducted this research project just at the time when the volume of priestly resignations began to increase spectacularly. The Second Vatican Council adjourned in December, 1965. One year later, just before Christmas, 1966, came the widely publicized announcement that Charles Davis, prominent British theologian and *peritus* at the Council, had abandoned both the priesthood and the Catholic Church and married Florence Henderson, a former American member of the Grail.[7] During 1967, and in subsequent years, an increasing number of men left the priestly ministry, most of them taking a wife in the process. Many among them, however, wanted both to marry and to continue in the active priestly ministry.

Pastoral Renewal

The group of St. Louis priests who originated and financed the clergy survey were convinced that the pastoral *aggiornamento* of the Roman Church has to include a married priesthood. Even before the survey findings were publicized they organized a program to keep the issue alive. An Advisory Board of volunteers, of which I was a member, included Robert Franceour, George Frein, Frank Matthews, Alfred McBride, and John O'Brien. In January, 1967, the Board announced the formal establishment of the National Association for Pastoral Renewal. Lay persons, including interested women, were invited to join but, for the most part, its members were Catholic priests. Some of them were "going steady" and on the verge of marriage, some had no intention to marry, but all had the conviction that the pastoral renewal of the Church must inevitably embrace the option for clergy to marry.

Aside from writing the constitution and bylaws, electing officers and absorbing large numbers of members, NAPR quickly set three projects in motion. The first of these was a proposal that a "vicariate" be canonically established in which married Catholic priests could carry on the active ministry under the jurisdiction of their own bishop.[8] This relatively novel ecclesiastical structure, called also a prelature or ordinariate, had its American model in the military vicariate, in which a member of the hierarchy has pastoral responsibility for all Catholic personnel in the military services of the United States. The Vatican Council had already approved the institution of "personal prelatures" where needed. (*Presbyterorum Ordinis*, art. 10) This proposal was submitted to Archbishop John Deardon, then President of the National Conference of Catholic Bishops, but it seems to have disappeared without a trace.

A second project had the double aim of replicating my earlier survey on clerical celibacy and marriage, and also attempting to obtain actual statistics on the numbers of priests who had resigned. The survey provided regional data that between fifty and sixty-five percent of diocesan priests favored optional marriage. The exact count of priestly resignees is still difficult to ascertain, although the declining "trends" have been traced by several sociologists.[9]

The third project was a symposium on clergy celibacy to be conducted in September, 1967, at the University of Notre Dame. Early in the Spring, the NAPR secretary, Robert Franceour, and the symposium chairman, George Frein, contacted the prospective program participants. Most of the NAPR membership were not yet married, but those who were married decided to stay discretely in the background, lest their presence arouse the ire of the hierarchy. In fact, every effort was made to attract attendance of some bishops to the Notre Dame Conference.[10] This expectation was shattered three months before the symposium, when Pope Paul VI issued his encyclical, *Sacerdotalis Coelibatus,* calling for continued adherence to priestly celibacy, the "brilliant jewel" of the Roman Church.

Almost as an afterthought, the Pope allowed a loophole for the possible admission of married clergy from non-Catholic denominations. While perpetual celibacy remains the rule for Roman priests, he suggested that "a study may be allowed of the particular circumstances of married sacred ministers of Churches, or other Christian communities, separated from the Catholic Communion, and of the possibility of admitting to priestly functions those who desire to adhere to the fullness of this Communion and to continue to exercise the sacred ministry." (*Sacerdotalis Caelibatus,* art. 42) The Pope cautions that the possible admittance of convert married priests "does not signify a relaxation of the existing law, and must not be interpreted as a prelude to its abolition." As a matter of fact, only thirteen years later, the door was opened to a limited number of married Episcopal priests.[11]

The Pope's message apparently fortified the reluctance of the American Bishops to deal with, or even to discuss, the question of optional marriage. To the disappointment of the sponsors, no American Bishop was in attendance at the Notre Dame Symposium, although all had been invited. "A few had sent regrets that they were busy, and a few said they doubted the sincerity of the sponsoring group." There were rumors that episcopal pressure was put on the President of Notre Dame University to cancel the use of the campus for the symposium. After the event, Bishop Leo Pursley, the local Ordinary of the diocese, complained that the "usual courtesies" had not been observed. He said he was informed of the symposium only after it had been scheduled, and that one of its chief promoters, Father John O'Brien of the Notre Dame faculty, had failed to hold "prior consultation" with the Ordinary.

The symposium attracted an attendance of 211 registered persons, received excellent radio and television coverage, and achieved nationwide publicity in both the secular and religious press. The chairman of the meeting, George Frein, edited the program papers for publication by Herder and Herder.[12] Subsequently, he too resigned from the priesthood and married.[13] Another man was quietly present at this symposium, the priest who started it all in the previous year when he proposed the research study and found the money to support it. On the day after the symposium ended, Frank Matthews announced to his parishioners in St. Louis that he was resigning the priesthood and the pastorate. He, too, soon took the option to marry.

Beyond Optional Marriage

As a member of the Advisory Board of NAPR, my interpretation of "pastoral renewal" seemed much broader than that of the leaders and the general membership. The most interested men and women were those who had already married, or who were practically engaged to marry, and all of them wanted to remain in the active ministry. I argued that lifting the prohibition against clerical marriage would have to be the opening to further change. All the other problems of institutionalized clericalism would still remain to be solved. "The shift to a voluntary married clergy would entail other changes: revision of residence for the multi-staff rectory; a new salary scale to assure an adequate family wage; a new design for recruitment and training of seminarians, and many other changes that are probably unforeseen."[14] I tested this prediction later, at a meeting with a group of resigned priests and their wives: "Would you return to the active priesthood, if you could bring your wives with you?"

The wives of these priests raised immediate objections, which were very similar to the complaints of Protestant ministers' wives: attitudes and expectations of parishioners; the confinement of rectory life; insufficient income; the professional demands on the time and energy of their priest-husbands.[15] Wives who had been nuns were enjoying married life "just as it is," with no great desire to go back into the clerical rigidities. The men themselves were more reflective of the entire institutionalized structure in the system of appointments and promotions; due process in grievances; opportunities for sabbaticals and continuing education; better communication with diocesan authorities, and a share in decision-making.

Journalists, commentators and interviewers seemed determined to make priest marriages the central issue of Church renewal. In Boston, in 1967, I participated in several "talk shows" on radio and television and had difficulty—in fact, was unable—to divert the "talk master's" attention off the question of married priests. After my book, *America's Forgotten Priests,* was published I was a guest on an afternoon television program in Cleveland—one of those shows on which the viewers are asked to call in their votes on the topic. The question, of which I was not even aware until the program had started, was: "Should Catholic Priests be Allowed to Marry?" Seventy-one percent of the 1,143 voters—probably mainly homemakers of various religious affiliations—called in affirmatively.

Meanwhile, NAPR, besides conducting its continuing surveys, attempting to get the ear of the hierarchy, and mailing out propaganda statements, was planning another symposium to be held at St. Louis University in September, 1968. Archbishop

Carberry was unhappy with university officials for allowing this meeting on the campus and also let it be known that he did not want his seminarians and priests to attend it. NAPR continued to be an annoyance to the hierarchy because it continued to center its efforts on the removal of the celibacy rule.

The NAPR meeting in St. Louis was notable for the fact that it gave birth to a new organization, the Society of Priests for a Free Ministry. I was present at the informal evening discussion during which this started and I felt that it was narrowing still further the concept of pastoral renewal throughout the ecclesiastical structure. The proponents of the new group were men who refused to accept their status as "ex-priests," on the insistence that marriage, or laicization, or even formal excommunication, could not remove the sacramental character bestowed on them by holy orders. Their "free" ministry at first meant freedom from canonical strictures, but some emphasized that they did not charge a stipend for their services. They were willing to support themselves, their wife, and family by gainful "secular" employment, but they were also ready to provide priestly ministry to anyone needing their spiritual services.

Eugene Bianchi, the first president, set the tone of SPFM in 1969 when he wrote that, "Catholicism is still too afflicted with the patterns of un-freedom." In an almost bellicose mood he said that, "the purpose of creative resistance movements is to analyze clearly the abusive power concentrations that maintain these un-freedoms."[16] He, Tom Durkin, and Bernard McGoldrick, drew the more restive members of NAPR into the SPFM. Their newsletter, *Diaspora*, explored an ever broader concept of the ministerial profession to include women and other hitherto non-ordained persons. In 1973 they made themselves into the Fellowship of Christian Ministry, which then included non-Catholic persons ready to do ministry in novel ways. One further name change was to the Federation of Christian Ministry, at which point they instituted a program of professional certification for the Christian ministry.

Some of the members who drifted away—Terrence Dosh, Thomas Durkin, Frank Bonnike, and others—constituted a kind of organizational link with the beginnings of CORPUS, which then remained more orthodox than the FCM. They sensed ecclesial danger in moving to the schismatic scheme for a free and open priesthood that would include ordained women and non-Catholic clergy. The "founders" of CORPUS had been active in the Association of Chicago Priests, and were unready to be either radicals or rebels. In 1974 an informal nucleus came together under the prodding of Frank Bonnike, Frank McGrath, and Bill Nemmers, and they modestly called themselves "facilitators" of the group. Over the years the "paper work" grew in correspondence with the increasing membership. Ten years later, in 1984, they hired Terry Dosh part-time as the executive secretary and coordinator of the group.

CORPUS as a Movement

The Corps of Reserve Priests United for Service (CORPUS) grew rapidly on the national scene and underwent a complete reorganization in the Fall of 1988, when they decided to call themselves the National Association for a Married Priesthood. The facilitators "passed the torch" to a newly constituted board of eleven members, with the nationally known theologian, Anthony Padovano as the first president. The central office was moved from Chicago to Minneapolis, with Terry Dosh as the full-time national coordinator. The reorganization included a network of regional coordinators around the country and the establishment of "branches" in more than seventy cities where efforts are made to develop friendly relations with the local bishop.

Unlike the disgruntled promoters of the Federation for Christian Ministry, the members of CORPUS adhered to the basic principle of cooperation with the hierarchy. The "apostolic succession" of bishops was the guarantee of validity of their holy orders and was not under dispute. They simply wanted the bishops to recognize married priests and their wives as potential allies and co-workers, not as radicals or rebels ready to embarrass Church officials. In short, they wanted to convince the bishops that they were still priests and ready to resume the active ministry. The facilitators reminded the Bishops' Committee on Priestly Life and Ministry that Pope John Paul II, in his recent Holy Thursday homily, recognized that men who resigned their canonical posts do remain priests. "These brother priests," said Paul VI, "unhappy or deserters as they may be— are marked with an indelible imprint of the Spirit which makes them priests for all eternity, whatever changes they may undergo outwardly or socially."[17] Most of the CORPUS members say, "I opt for marriage, not for resignation from the priesthood."

Meanwhile, the movement of married priests' associations was developing in Europe. In a sense, the Dutch clergy led the way in attempting to retain married priests in the diocesan parishes. The Holy Father called the Dutch Bishops to Rome for a much publicized Synod in 1980, which reiterated that priests are not allowed to have wives. To fortify this position in Holland, he appointed known conservative prelates to several dioceses. Then, in 1985 the First International Assembly of Married Priests was held at Ariccia, Italy, not far from Rome. Approximately 200 married priests and their wives attended, from fifteen countries, including a large contingent from the United States.

These international contacts and experiences foreshadowed the First National Conference of CORPUS, held in June, 1988, at American University in Washington, D.C. It was an efficiently programmed and well-received conference, the result of competent advance planning. This national meeting represented a kind of rebirth, a transition from a volatile social movement to an efficient social organization. Facilitator Frank McGrath had made the observation that, "from the beginning CORPUS was defined as a movement, not an organization—no officers, no structure, no meetings—just an idea, a reality, a manifestation of a shared priesthood still very much alive." The official transition from a loose informal movement to a well-structured organization was verified at the first national meeting in Washington. As Terry Dosh remarked, "Nineteen Eighty-eight is the year of the quantum leap for CORPUS. It is the year when a big jump in public consciousness can occur."

The Second National Conference of CORPUS was held in 1989, at Columbus, Ohio, on the Campus of Capital University. This year, the conference theme was "Companions on a Journey," with the subtitle, "People of God Affirm a Married Priesthood." The Third Annual Conference, held in 1990 on the Campus of San Jose State University, met under the slogan, "Priestless Sundays." CORPUS had now expanded, more than doubling its dues-paying membership, which includes unmarried priests, interested lay persons and other well-wishers. Yet, it has been consistent in maintaining the orthodox ecclesiastical principles with which it started. CORPUS has remained strongly Roman Catholic and is not in any way a movement of rebellious secession.

Participating Wives

From the beginning, the main problem with married priests, and the thing that bothers the bishops most, was that they had wives. Other priests and prelates, and many of the Catholic laity, did not know how to act, or react, to the presence of wives of priests. It was thought best to keep them in the background. In the beginnings of CORPUS, as one wife complained, "we were just like baggage that was being dragged along when our husbands wanted to get reinstated. We were just an adjective, a detail, in the process." CORPUS had but a single purpose and it had nothing to do with the feminist movement, women's liberation, or the ordination of women. Like most of the Catholic clergy, even the married priests were heavily into clericalism and sexism.

Nevertheless, Frank McGrath later reminisced that, "the wives of the CORPUS facilitators were most important right from the beginning; no meeting or activity occurred without their input and contributions. It was Janet Bonnike who came up with the acronym, CORPUS, and Joan Wilbur who designed the logo."[18] This feminine initiative was not widely known. In fact, even the founding facilitators kept themselves anonymous and could be reached at first only through a post office box in Chicago. That was in 1974, when the quiet beginnings of the movement proceded with utmost caution. At this point, however, CORPUS contracted for a Gallup poll that revealed a majority of lay Catholics willing to accept a married clergy, a "discovery" that had been made a decade earlier in our sociological surveys.

Meanwhile, some of the wives were becoming restive in the role of silent supporters of their husbands. One of the "veteran" wives complained in 1984 that "some of the leaders tend to overlook women and don't consider even the possibility that wives have good ideas and should be included in positions of leadership." Nevertheless, she insisted that "you can't generalize about them. The wives of priests are like any other wives. There's no pattern that describes them. Some work closely with the husband-priests and support their effort to regain access to ministry. Some wives are uninterested in the priest-side of their husbands, or even openly oppose any ministry."

Women were finally given the opportunity to raise their voices at the First National Conference on the Married Priesthood held on the non-Catholic Campus of American University in Washington. The three-day program included a session on the theme that, "Mandatory Celibacy is Starving the Catholic Community," which was presented by nine speakers, two of whom were women. It was, however, in the several dialogue workshops that the wives began to make their presence felt. As a result, one of the "Directions" agreed upon at this conference was that CORPUS "affirms the right and inspiration of women to full participation in all ministries of the Church, and asserts solidarity with those who are moving to open these ministries to women."

The survey questionnaire I distributed in 1989 elicited responses from some wives who were disgruntled at the conservativism of their men and who refused to remain anonymous. "If the primary aim of CORPUS is the reinstatement of a previously ordained, married male clergy, then there is clearly no place for women short of hollow support and acknowledgement. Women are reduced to an auxiliary function, as is reflected today in the Church. This position is most detrimental to our cause, in that it convicts us of the same sin of patriarchy that we are currently being oppressed by." Such protest at the Washington Conference brought about two demands: One was the admission of women to "full membership" in CORPUS; the second was the election of women to the Board of Directors.

Another outspoken wife who attended the International Congress at Ariccia, Italy, in 1987, as well as the National Meeting at Washington the following summer, came to the bold conclusion that "there is little or no place in the structure of CORPUS for men and women who believe in a discipleship of equals, and who wish to spend their best energies toward this goal." She was disheartened that less than half of the married priests favor the ordination of women, and she asked: "Why not explore the gifts women bring to a wounded Church rather than to a married priesthood? Why not work together in equality to 'package, promote and sell' women's gifts to the Church with the same vigor the brothers are marketing their own?"

This kind of complaint, voiced also by other wives, was not lost on the CORPUS leaders in preparation for the Second Annual Conference, held in June, 1989, at Capital University, Columbus, Ohio. Prime attention was here focused on the priests' wives with the convention slogan: "Companions on a Journey: People of God Affirm a Married Priesthood." It was significant that five of the nine featured speakers were women. The hesitation about female leadership was finally absolved at the Columbus meeting, with the election of two wives, Ann O'Brien and Linda Pinto, to the "Collegial Board."

The Third National CORPUS meeting was also held on a non-Catholic campus, the State University of San Jose, California. A dialogue panel was "anchored" by Susan Secora and featured three outspoken feminists, Ann Bukovchic, Phyllis Soto, and Barbara Barry. All four are the wives of priests and while they want their husbands reinstated in the ministry, they want a restructuring of the Church that excludes sexism, clericalism and patriarchalism. Much of the ensuing discussion revolved around the preference between married priests and women priests from the perspective of sequence. They were aware that the answer lies with the hierarchy who happened to be meeting on the same days at nearby Santa Clara University. After this panel, and at the invitation of the bishops, the participants bussed to the Campus of Santa Clara to dialogue with a subcommittee of bishops.

A kind of "conflict of interest" erupted when the CORPUS members conducted a prayer service in front of the campus chapel at the very time that a group of ardent feminists foregathered to promote women's ordination. They called themselves the "Women's Ministry Dialogue," having originated at the Berkeley School of Theology. They scheduled a vesper service that was meant to attract the bishops' attention to the acceptance of women to the Catholic priesthood. Some of their members complained that their demand for women's ordination had been minimized by the CORPUS promotion of the married priesthood.

Another group of women, a very small number, came to the San Jose Conference with a different proposal. They wanted special attention given to married women who have a divine calling to the priesthood. Their argument was that if married men were allowed to be priests, then equal consideration should be given to married women. There was also a growing minority of priests' wives who felt the stirrings of priestly vocation, but these were quite different from the married women who had a call to ordination with no reference to their husbands.[19] It is understandable, of course, that the CORPUS leadership could not take them seriously.

The Friendly Bishops

The 1990 Conference of Married Priests at San Jose constituted a kind of "breakthrough" in their relationships with the hierarchy. Since departing the active ministry, many of the resigned priests had had some contact with the episcopacy, usually their own Ordinary. They have been deliberately cautious, both individually and collectively, to avoid antagonistic confrontations. As in previous years, the coordinator invited every bishop in the country to attend the annual conference. It was a coincidence in 1990 that the National Conference of Catholic Bishops was holding its semi-annual meeting in the same weekend, June 22-24, at the nearby Santa Clara University. Two days before the meeting, reports Terry Dosh, "the bishops invited us to talk with them. We spent more than an hour with Bishops Donald Wuerl from Pittsburgh, Pierre Dumain of San Jose, John Favalora of Tampa, and John Marshall of Burlington."[20]

At the end of their prayer service on Saturday afternoon, June 23, the CORPUS group conducted an "inscription ceremony," in which married priests "were invited to come forward and sign a scroll, committing themselves for priestly service on the condition that discussions with their bishops will resolve issues of family commitments, employment, income, and parish receptivity, to questions of church and ministerial reform." In the early afternoon they brought the scroll to the Santa Clara Campus in "an activity of prayer and pilgrimage, to share the riches of CORPUS with the American Bishops."

The CORPUS representatives asked the bishops for two concessions: "first, that the organization could maintain ongoing contact with the Bishops' Committee on Priestly Life and Ministry, and secondly, that at some time in the near future they be allowed an opportunity to make a presentation to the whole assembled NCCB. These requests seemed reasonable to the bishops. Although this was the first time they had made direct contact with the officers of CORPUS, they had long been aware of the ultimate goal of these married priests: that they be reinstated in the company of their wives into the active canonical ministry of the Church. Meanwhile, they suggest that resigned priests be employed by the bishops where the needs are greatest—in rural missions, chaplaincies, specialized ministries—which could be done like the "tentmakers" who are financially stable.

The experience of Frank Bonnike is well-known and portrays such a ministry, at a time when the Archdiocese of Chicago was unable to fill eight hospital chaplaincies. From 1974 to 1984 he was emergency-room chaplain in the crisis ministry of Lutheran General Hospital. "It is my conviction," he says, "after ten years of living the life of a married man and a hospital chaplain, that there should be a married priest-chaplain in almost every hospital. Some would be full-time; others could work a night or two a week; some could simply be on call from their homes on emergencies."[21] The sacramental advantage for the sick and dying is that the validly ordained resigned priest could provide the sacraments of reconciliation and final anointing.

While no solid generalizations can be made about the changing attitudes of the American hierarchy—especially as more conservative prelates are being made bishops—there is wide evidence of more humane and Christ-like attitudes toward the resigned and married clergy. In the testimony of priests' wives we have heard both praise and blame. Some have been shunned by the local Ordinary; others report remarkable friendliness. In many instances there has been a shift from cold and legalistic rigidity to informal and friendly relationships.

Endnotes

1. Michael Novak, *The Open Church*, New York, Macmillan, 1964, p. 123.

2. Joseph H. Fichter, *America's Forgotten Priests*, New York, Harper & Row, 1968, pp. 162-166.

3. At that time I was Chauncey Stillman Professor at Harvard and long-time member of the *NCR* Board of Directors.

4. This "committee" did not materialize. Bishop Leven was promoted to Ordinary of the San Angelo Diocese in 1969. In the same year, Bishop Shannon took the option to marry and was formally excluded from the Church.

5. Joseph H. Fichter, *One-Man Research*, New York, Wiley, 1973, p. 179. See also, "That Celibacy Survey," *America*, January 21, 1967, pp. 92-94.

6. *The Catholic Priest in the United States: Sociological Investigation*, Washington, USCC, 1972, p. 239.

7. Charles Davis explained his position and decision in *A Question of Conscience*, New York, Harper & Row, 1967.

8. Perhaps the best-known personal prelature is *Opus Dei*, officially erected in 1982 by Pope John Paul II.

9. See Dean Hoge, *The Future of Catholic Leadership: Responses to the Priest Shortage*, Kansas City, Sheed & Ward, 1987, pp. 11-13.

10. These preparations are described in the "Introduction," pp. 7-17, in George Frein, ed., *Celibacy, The Necessary Option*, New York, Herder and Herder, 1968.

11. Joseph H. Fichter, *The Pastoral Provisions: Married Catholic Priests*, Kansas City, Sheed & Ward, 1989.

12. My symposium paper is included, "Sociology and Clerical Celibacy," pp. 102-122.

13. He tells his experience, "For the Love of Jeanne," pp. 85-88, in John A. O'Brien, ed., *Why Priests Leave,* New York, Hawthorn, 1969. For another case, see Cornelius Outcault, "A Good Young Priest," pp. 2-11 in James F. Colaianni, ed., *Married Priests and Married Nuns*, New York, McGraw-Hill, 1968.

14. *America's Forgotten Priests, op. cit.,* p. 210.

15. William Douglas, *Ministers' Wives*, New York, Harper & Row, 1965, chapter 4, "Fulfillments and Frustrations."

16. Eugene Bianchi, "Resistance in the Church," *Commonweal*, May 16, 1969.

17. "Reflections on the Last Supper," Holy Thursday Homily of Pope Paul VI (April 8, 1971), *The Pope Speaks,* vol. 16-17, 1971-72, pp. 8-12.

18. Frank McGrath, "Women and CORPUS," in *CORPUS Reports*, July 25, 1988.

19. In an earlier survey, Fran Ferder found five percent married and two percent divorced among the women "called to priesthood." *Called To Break Bread?* Mt. Rainier, Quixote Center, 1978, p. 33.

20. The media later reported that Bishop Wuerl had received a "scolding" letter from the Vatican. The Bishop said it was private correspondence simply requesting "information" about the meeting.

21. Frank Bonnike, *Camillian*, October, 1984.

Chapter Five

Wives of Catholic Deacons

Up until recently Roman Catholic deacons did not have wives because their ordination to the diaconate was a stepping stone on the way to the celibate priesthood. This *transitional* diaconate still exists for future priests, but the opening to the *permanent* diaconate for married men was made by the Fathers of the Second Vatican Council. "At a lower level of the hierarchy," they declared, "are deacons upon whom hands are imposed, not unto the priesthood, but unto a ministry of service." (*Lumen Gentium*, art. 29) These married deacons are the only Roman Catholics who are likely recipients of all seven sacraments. They receive the sacrament of holy orders so that they may "serve the People of God in the ministry of the liturgy, of the word, and of charity."

The permanent diaconate can be conferred "even upon those living in the married state," but they need a special Vatican dispensation to remarry if the wife dies. The law of celibacy is imposed on unmarried men who may be ordained deacon at the age of thirty-five years. The inclusion of married deacons in the hierarchy is a novelty only in modern times and only in the Latin Church. When St. Paul sent a salutation "to all the saints in Christ Jesus who are at Philippi, with the bishops and the deacons" (Phil. 1:1), there is no reason to think he was addressing only celibate clerics, at either the episcopal or diaconate level. There appears to be no specific mention of deacons' wives in the Acts of the Apostles, but it is most likely that some of the women described in the Acts and in Paul's epistles would have been married to deacons.

We need not be distracted here by the debates that continue to rage over the presence or absence of authentic deaconesses in the early centuries of the Church. In the letter to the Romans, Paul "commends our sister, Phoebe, a deaconess of the Church at Cenchrae." (Rom. 16:1) In later centuries the Byzantine ritual for the ordination of deaconesses required that they pronounce a vow of chastity.[1] Joan Morris admits that, "there was no question of women being ordained priests, but that from apostolic times deaconesses formed an order in the administration of the Church into which women were formally initiated by the laying on of hands."[2]

The focus of the Catholic Women's Ordination Conference continues to be on the priesthood, which implies the preliminary transitional diaconate for women. At the Second Conference in 1978, however, they passed a recommendation to "call upon the official Roman Catholic Church to recognize God's call to women to be permanent deacons."[3] A decade later, April, 1988, the American Bishops seriously considered this proposal. They praised the many women who serve in the pastoral ministry and who accomplish "many of the functions performed by ordained deacons and are capable of accomplishing all of them. The question of women being formally installed in the permanent diaconate arises quite naturally and pastoral reasons prompt its evaluation."[4]

Lumen Gentium, of Vatican II, which revived the permanent diaconate for males, was promulgated on November 21, 1964, but was not immediately activated by the American hierarchy. Without waiting for the initiative of bishops around the world, Pope Paul VI issued his Apostolic letter, Sacrum Diaconatus Ordinem, in 1967, which officially restored the clerical ordination of permanent deacons. In the following year, the American Bishops established formation programs in thirteen dioceses, that called for two years of training of the diaconal candidate. Out of this experience, even before the ordination of any deacons, came the provisional Guidelines, published in 1971.[5]

Little was said about the deacon's wife, except that no candidate could be accepted unless his wife gave formal consent to his application. The deacon's priorities were carefully spelled out: his first commitment to wife and family; secondly, to his gainful employment to sustain his family; and thirdly, to the obligations of the ministry itself. It was not clear how the wife was to share in her husband's ministry, but she was given every encouragement to participate in some concomitant training and formation.

The Wives Speak

The deacons' wives who provided the data for this enquiry live in a diocese of 145 parishes, of which only 75 are served by deacons. The diocesan *Directory* for 1990 lists the names and addresses of 150 deacons. Since we are focusing only on the wives of active deacons, we subtracted from the listing the names of the unmarried and widowed, the retired, those on leave, or on duty outside the diocese. This left a total of 128 deacons' wives, of whom we were able to contact and question 109 (85%). They are distributed in all eight ordination "classes," starting with the first group in 1974 and concluding with the Class of 1989. On the average, they have had 6.1 years in this diaconal relationship, besides the several years of association in the formation program.

These informants cannot be styled a representative sample of married Catholic women of the diocese. With some few exceptions, they tend to be from the comfortable middle class and more than half had some college education. They range in age from 39 to 79 years of age, with the average age at 54.3 years. From a growing population of Hispanic Catholics, less than five percent of the wives are of Hispanic background. From a diocese that contains 95,000 Black Catholics, less than ten percent of the deacons' wives are African-Americans.[6]

These women differ in attitudes and experiences according to their age and education and the length of time they have been associated in the diaconal program; but one of the few opinions on which they have almost complete agreement (93%) is that they themselves have no desire to be ordained deaconesses. They are unanimously proud of their husbands and are overwhelmingly convinced that their husbands' homilies are as good as those of the average priest. If there is a single flaw in their diaconal experience upon which almost all agree, it is in the negative attitudes of the parish priests toward them and their husbands. Those who venture an explanation of this negativism suggest that many of the priests are in the grip of both sexism and clericalism.

Formation

The preparatory, or "training" program, in which the wives of deacons are urged to participate has become longer and more elaborate. The earliest ordination classes in the diocese (1974 and 1976) went through the program in two years, with no preliminary process of discernment and without a semester of Clinical Pastoral Training. In those early years relatively few (16%) of the wives attended all, or most, of the classes, as compared to half of the wives in recent years. The contemporary formation program extends for three years (CIC 236) and is anticipated by three so-called "discernment" sessions over a period of several months. These are meetings at which the prospective candidate and his wife are introduced to the theory and practice of the permanent diaconate.

The names of potential candidates are usually submitted by the parish priests and may number in the scores. The popularity of the permanent diaconate can be estimated by the large number of aspirants, but elimination, or "de-selection," thins out the ranks. The discernment process subjects these men and their wives to official diocesan scrutiny and allows the applicant couple to examine their own qualifications. The number of aspirants is sharply reduced during this preliminary screening process. Some are afraid of the required academic studies and drop out. Regularly there are men who withdraw because their wives object to the stipulation that widowed deacons may not remarry.

The wives are present at every step of the discernment process, are themselves screened, and are conscientiously examined for their attitudes and opinions. These group meetings are held at the diocesan seminary and in some years more than two-thirds of the prospective candidates are eliminated. It is at this point that the surviving couples are permitted to fill out the application form. Now a further investigation takes place in the form of three interviews in the couple's home. These home visits are conducted by one of the priests as well as by an experienced deacon couple.

In the diocese under study the earliest classes (1974 and 1976) were conducted according to the 1971 *Guidelines,* which had been produced "from a wish to assist the establishment of the diaconate in this country but could not reflect actual experience, since they were written before any permanent deacons were ordained." In this sense the first two deacon classes were experimental, with the faculty and administration ready to make changes and improvements. While the wives were allowed to attend the instructions, the priest teachers ignored their presence in the classroom. Only two wives attended all the classes, one of whom told us, "in the beginning I didn't feel really welcomed in the classes." The great majority (76%) said they did not attend any classes at all with their husbands. There were twelve men ordained in the first class and fourteen in the second. "After the '76 class was ordained," said the Deacon Director, "we changed the screening process, asked for more specific references, and insisted that the wife had to be involved in every step of the formation process."

According to the revised Code of Canon Law (CIC 236), the formation program must last at least three years and some of the deacons think of it as a kind of "mini-seminary" education. The integrated program, in which the wives share, emphasizes not only theological knowledge, but also pastoral and spiritual formation. In this city, and in urban areas generally, the program turns out to be a night school, meeting twice weekly for three-hour sessions. In each of the semesters, husband and wife attend a day of spiritual reflection, and in the summers, between the spring and fall semesters, they are expected to attend a retreat with other deacon couples. Since the Class of 1983 a seventh semester has been added, a thirteen-week program in Clinical Pastoral Training, which is not required of the wives.

In subsequent ordination classes the attendance of wives increased notably in the formation program. While the Bishop has not made the attendance of wives mandatory, a certain degree of social pressure is brought to bear on them. They all make good resolutions at the beginning of the three-year training period, but the wives' attendance gradually tapers off, especially if there are young children in the family. "At that time our youngsters were still pre-school, and when I could not get to class he taped it and we listened to it together; so I heard all the classes." It may be noted here that about two out of five (39%) of the wives feel that a father should not apply for the diaconate program if he has children still in elementary or secondary school. The Director, however, thinks that fathers now have to pay more attention to teenagers than to younger children.

As a spiritual and familial preliminary to the life of clerical marriage some of the wives and husbands participated together in Marriage Encounter (59%), in the Charismatic Renewal (48%), and in the Cursillo Movement (28%). These background experiences suggest that the candidate and his wife were more than ordinarily devout and loyal Catholics prepared to follow the obligations incumbent on a new and ministerial way of life.

Ordination

The men who survive the discernment process and successfully pursue the program of theological, pastoral and spiritual formation, are not automatically accepted for ordination. In compliance with the revised Code of Canon Law they must be installed for two preliminary ministries as reader and acolyte (no longer called "minor orders"). After the third semester of the formation program they take on the ministry of reader, which means that they may read the first two lessons of the Mass, from the Old and New Testaments. After the fifth semester they are installed in the ministry of acolyte. Recently ordained deacons claim that they are not so attracted to this as were the veterans. "We were told that we had to be installed as acolytes, a canonical step toward the diaconate. I would say that 95% of the class did not want to wear the alb as acolyte. They prefer not to wear liturgical garments."[7]

The wife's required public assent to her husband's diaconal ordination had in previous years been given in the midst of the ordination ceremony itself. This testimony has now been moved to a candidacy meeting prior to the ordination Mass. The wife swears a solemn oath in the presence of witnesses, in which she says: "I do hereby give my consent to his ordination in pursuance of Canon 1050 of the Code of Canon Law. I further attest that I do so with a clear understanding of the specific obligation attached to this order and with my own free will, motivated by no consideration other than the glory of God and the service of the Church of the diocese. I make this agreement under oath, as I touch the Book of Sacred Scripture."

All the preparatory training culminates in the ordination Mass in early December, preceded by a spiritual retreat and by a prayer vigil, when the Bishop gives a final exhortation. He stresses the significance of mutual support and cooperation, and urges the women to continue sharing in their husband's ministry. The wives should be comfortable in working with their husbands, and provide a necessary support in the ministry. He repeats what they had often already heard: that the deacon's priorities are first to wife and family, second to gainful employment, and thirdly to the actual ministry. One wife remarked that "he made it sound so wonderful, but that's not the way it goes. For three and a half years it was diaconate first, then job, then family." This was verified by the husband who said that "if you missed a class because of your job, the excuse was acceptable, but if it was because of some family emergency that was not an acceptable excuse."

The ordination Mass itself is a sacred experience for the married couple, but in the opinion of some wives the "revised" ceremony tends to separate rather than unite the couple. In the new Code the ordination ceremony for the permanent married deacon is exactly the same as that for the transitional celibate deacon. One of the "older" wives complained that "what is happening now is that the wife is shoved aside." She described her own earlier experience: "We walked into the Cathedral with our husbands and sat in the same pews with them. They were in albs. We held the stole and dalmatics with which we vested them. At a certain point the wives stood and gave our permission publicly as part of the ceremony. When it came time to leave we formed a procession with them."[9]

All this has been changed. The call from the family has been separated out; the vesting is done by a deacon or a priest. The ordination rite is pointed specifically at the diaconal ritual, oblivious to the fact that the primary sacrament of the deacon is matrimony. It is an interesting fact that some bishops have not made these adaptations and insist that marriage makes the ceremony of the permanent diaconate different from that of the transitional diaconate. This apparent devaluation of wives and marriage has led some bishops in Canada and the United States to suspend completely the deacon formation program.

Ministry

During the years of formation and training, wives were regularly encouraged to plan for their own partnership in their husband's ministry. Six out of ten (63%) said that this had been their expectation. They had often discussed with their husbands the manner in which they might work together in his ministry. It appears, however, that these promises and expectations do not work out successfully. Only one-third report that they share "fully" or a "great deal" in his ministry and this participation is much higher (54%) among the more recently ordained. "We wives were all involved with the program. Then came ordination day, and they were ordained. Now they are going on to do their ministry, and here we are. That was some sort of a letdown."

Every deacon—like the priests—is ordained for the diocese, and not for the parish. Yet, every deacon must be "attached to an altar" (the parish church), which is meant to validate the liturgical aspect of his ministry. It is the bishop who makes her husband's parochial assignment. The pastor is expected to come to some arrangement about the deacon's duties: frequency of preaching, of baptismal preparation, attendance at wakes. These are not always clearly spelled out.[8] "They are pretty fuzzy," says one wife, "because the pastor doesn't seem to know what he wants the deacon to do." When the commitment is made to the assigned parish, the wife countersigns her acceptance of the memorandum of understanding; which is signed also by the pastor and the director of the permanent diaconate.

Except for a few complaints the wives are generally "supportive" of their deacon husbands, but there is an essential difference between *supporting* the diaconal ministry and actually *participating* in it. The liturgical assignment "to an altar" is never allowed to a woman. Thus, the complete service of the People of God in liturgy, in word, and in charity, can be the total commitment of only the deacon, not of his wife. It was the husband who was solemnly installed to the ministry of preacher, "to proclaim God's word in the midst of his people." He was accepted into the ministry of acolyte "to serve at the altar and assist the presbyter, particularly during Mass." In all the ceremonies preparatory to ordination, and at the ordination itself, there was never any suggestion that the wife is to function in the diaconal ministry, even as a kind of surrogate deaconess.

The gender distinction is never so clear as at Sunday Mass, when the husband, in alb and stole, is in the sanctuary while his wife sits alone in the pews. In August, 1972, when Pope Paul abolished the sub-diaconate, minor orders and tonsure, he established the new ministries of lector and acolyte. These ministries are "open to lay persons but are restricted at this time to men." The fact is that this restriction is not fully observed in this diocese. A minority of deacons' wives (24%) say that they regularly "do the readings." Some are "temporarily appointed" to do the acolyte function of carrying the sacramentary, the processional cross and candles. Half of them are extraordinary ministers of the Eucharist, distributing Holy Communion at Mass, as well as to the sick and elderly.

In the early years of the permanent diaconate in this diocese the wives were often proud that their husbands were identified by wearing clerical attire. Some of the older deacons feel it is proper that they should thus be identified as clergy persons. There had already been six diaconal ordination classes when the Bishop, in June 1986, banned the wearing of clerical attire. "One of the gifts of the permanent diaconate," he wrote, "is its identification with the ordinary life-style of the faith community from which the deacon comes and continues to live. His calling is to share the daily common life experience with his sisters and brothers in the Lord. For pastoral reasons it is essential that he continue to identify closely with the faithful, even in his public attire."

The bishop's official prohibition was a response to the revised Code of Canon Law of 1983, wherein permanent deacons were no longer bound by the prescriptions of clerical dress (Can. 284). One of the commentators on the revised Code remarked that "it seems incongruous to some to exempt from clerical obligations those who were clerics." One of the veteran deacons complained half-seriously, "we've been defrocked by the Bishop." One of the younger deacons, however, thinks it is better for deacons not to be confused with priests. "At best we are not even mini-priests. We can't hear confessions or give the last sacraments."[9]

Everybody knows that permanent deacons are not ordained to the priesthood and their wives are not ordained to the diaconate. When we asked the wives if they would like to see their husbands ordained to the priesthood the large majority (71%) answered in the negative. It may be noted that the veteran wives are less negative (48%) than the wives (91%) of more recently ordained. We asked also if they themselves would like to be ordained to the diaconate and again the negative response came from the majority (93%). Finally, we asked whether the Church should ordain women to the diaconate and got agreement from only a minority (19%). It is probably safe to suggest that there are not many militant feminists among these wives.

Most of the wives have a deep interest and concern about the preaching experiences of their husbands and the great majority are ready to agree that "deacons' homilies are generally as good as priests' homilies." The frequency of preaching depends upon the decision of the pastor and about half the deacons preach on a regular monthly basis; three out of ten more than once a month, and the remainder are "seldom or never" in the pulpit. The wives' appraisal is expected to be subjective and perhaps biased, but they report that their husbands spend many hours in the preparation of sermons and in most cases rehearse the script with them. Several confess that they "get nervous" when they listen to their husband in the pulpit or watch him conduct services like baptisms, weddings, wakes, and funerals.

Ministry of Wives

During the formation period and in the several ceremonies leading to ordination, the wives were exhorted to share the ministry of their husbands. This exhortation had to be tailored to both the permissions and prohibitions of the Code of Canon Law. "Even though it is clearly understood from the outset that the wife is not to be ordained, nevertheless, her marriage and family are truly involved." The *Guidelines* then advise (110) that "the nurturing and deepening of their mutual sacrificial love will be the most important way that she will be involved in her husband's public ministry in the Church."

In 1988 the U. S. Bishops went further than this in recommending that the diaconal office should be seriously considered for women and that "women participate in all liturgical ministries that do not require ordination." In the same vein, they encouraged "the theological preparation of women to preach the Gospel and to use their gifts as preachers in the Church."[10] In 1990 they recommended that the question of the diaconate for women "be submitted to thorough investigation."[11] The bishops say also that many women "want expanded opportunities for ministry. A significant number are convinced that the ordination of women to ministerial priesthood is the only way to attain full participation in the Church."

Attendance at the academic lectures and spiritual exercises of the diaconal program over the course of six semesters produces a special category of women who are competent for the normal tasks of the diaconal ministry. Approximately four out of ten (43%) report that they attended "all" or "almost all" of the classes with their husbands. From the perspective of religious education this earned them certification as instructor at the elementary school level. With a few further academic courses they may be certified for teaching religion at the high-school level. About six out of ten (58%) report that they do participate in their parochial Confraternity of Christian Doctrine and RCIA.

In the normal urban parish there are many opportunities of ministries in which both husband and wife participate. Together they hold seminars for the instruction of expectant parents. They are particularly helpful to the pastor who is preparing engaged couples for marriage. They may alternate prayers and lead the rosary at a wake service. They hold prayer vigils in nursing homes and for shut-in sick and elderly persons. One couple took the Clinical Pastoral Training together and have a joint ministry as chaplains in a Protestant hospital. Another instance is that of a deacon in full-time prison ministry, in which his wife provides full mutual support.

In most parishes the deacon's wife has only limited access to the first two diaconal commitments: ministry of the liturgy and ministry of the word. There is great and expanding opportunity, however, in the ministry of charity, of looking after the social welfare of the People of God. Everyone knows that the Apostles chose seven men and ordained them to handle the welfare needs of the growing number of the faithful. (Acts 6:1) This was the all-consuming activity that initiated the order of deacons in the early Church. The typical parochial outreach for the works of charity is the St. Vincent de Paul Society, which is thought of as a men's group; but several deacons have expanded and transformed the group to include women, in which the deacon's wife is actively engaged.

Even without ordination, or a specific assignment from the bishop, women have borne the brunt of this Christian social commitment all through the centuries. The bishops themselves remarked that "women not only continue to carry the bulk of everyday work in the parish; they are also renewing the Church's tradition of feminine spirituality as a source of inspiration and growth."[12] In a sense, the wives of deacons are continuing, augmenting, replacing, the tasks that communities of religious women have traditionally performed in Catholic social welfare. Even without benefit of ordination or religious vows, women are everywhere more numerous than men in the social ministries of the Church.

There is no respondent to this survey who says that she "does nothing" in the parish. It is not surprising that they are readily available to do at least part-time secretarial work in the parish rectory and that they tend to be the "lay Apostles" of the parish. They are the "reliables" without whom the parish would lose much of its apostolic effectiveness. Approximately half (52%) of the deacons' wives are gainfully employed; about one-fifth are at home with children or taking care of elderly parents. Like their deacon husbands, they are "in the part-time service" of the Church.

In the midst of the busy diaconal ministry, the wives sometimes have to remind their husbands that the primary commitment of the diaconate is to wife and family. "If he were out playing golf or fishing, I could complain, but it makes me feel guilty when I put family before his ministry." Another wife complained that "sometimes he is called at the last minute, without thought to family commitments." Still another remarked, "I wish he had waited till retirement to do this."

Deacons are advised officially that they should best serve about ten hours per week. In the present study the wives report that their husbands dedicate an average of 12.4 hours per week to the ministry. This average excludes the three deacons who work full-time for the diocese. It does, however, represent an enormous spread between one-fifth who work five hours or less per week and the busiest one-fifth category who work twenty or more hours per week. Although the large majority (82%) of the wives of the present study deny that his ministry takes "too much time" away from home, they tend to be ambivalent under further questioning. As one wife commented, "with his meetings and appointments and homily preparations, it's hard to see him working the equivalent of eight days a week." In a less exaggerated tone, another remarked that "sometimes it interferes with my plans, and he never says no when asked to do something."

A further note of marital and diaconal cooperation lies in the advice given them by their spiritual counselor that they attend specified days of spirituality together, and especially to make the annual spiritual retreat. We asked if they had fulfilled this spiritual exercise during the previous twelve months. Approximately half (52%) answered affirmatively, but the readiness to fulfill this counsel appears to lag over the years. The wives in the veteran couples are much less likely (29%) than those of the more recently ordained (77%) to report that they had fulfilled this spiritual expectation.

Relations with Priests

Previous studies of the permanent diaconate have revealed that the most frustrating aspect of the diaconal experience is their unsatisfactory relationship with priests. In an earlier national survey among 150 bishops who had had direct experience with deacons, we learned that seven out of ten (69%) detected "conflict between deacons and priests."[13] This episcopal observation is further sustained by the respondents to this survey, among whom a large proportion (80%) agree that "some priests tend to look down on deacons." One wife told sadly of the "disappointment in my husband in not being accepted as a member of the clergy and staff." Another wife admitted that she herself felt "hurt and humiliation because some priests have no compassion for deacons."

There are indeed some vocal priests in the diocese who say that the deacons "pretend to be priests" and that the whole formation program is aimed at the "clericalization of the laity." One of the veteran deacons who regrets the prohibition against wearing the Roman collar complains that "the average priest, including some of the Jesuits I know, do not include us as clerics. And they don't want you on the altar." Later he added that "there is only one weakness in the structure of the Church concerning deacons. That's the relationship between the average priest and the deacons. Most priests, for some reason, fear the diaconate, and I don't know why."

Since every deacon is "assigned to an altar" by the Bishop there must obviously be some level of working relations between the deacon and the parish priests. Not every pastor wants a deacon connected to his parish. This has to be a partial explanation why about half of the 145 parishes in the diocese are without the assistance of a deacon. No pastor is obliged to sign up a deacon, and the decision to exclude the deacon is not otherwise easy to explain. The presence or absence of a deacon does not seem to depend on the size or the wealth of a parish, or the racial composition of its members. For some unexplained reason the parishes with diocesan priest pastors are more likely (54% to 34%) than religious order parishes to have deacons. The suburban parishes are more likely (55%) than the city parishes (40%) to have deacons, even multiple deacons.

The wives are very aware of the strained relations between their husbands and the priests and they have a suspicion that they themselves may be the reason for the priests' dislike. As one wife noted: "Some clergy have difficulty in accepting the role of the deacon, and it is even more rare for a priest to accept the ministry of a deacon and his wife." We probed the question on this matter. What are the attitudes of pastors to the wives of deacons? A fairly large minority (44%) of the wives are convinced that pastors "really don't know how to deal with the wives of deacons." About three out of ten (31%) say that pastors "fail to utilize the talents of deacons' wives." There is yet a minority (17%) who think that pastors would "prefer the help of celibate deacons."

In the light of such observations we may well note the concern of the American Bishops who perceive "the dismay of Catholic women when priests accept them merely as sacristans or caterers of parish receptions."[14] The *Guidelines* for the diaconate suggest a "catechesis of the presbyterate" (122) which may well include instructions on the avoidance of clericalism and sexism. The bishops went so far as to declare that "an incapacity to deal with women as equals should be considered a negative indication for fitness for ordination." There can be no question that the cooperative relationship of priests and women is to the advantage of the Church ministry. "When priests respect women and uphold their gifts, women are inclined to respond with a fresh desire to contribute; when the opposite occurs, joy and hope tend to corrode."[15]

Relations with the Laity

Leonard Doohan reminds us that "some bishops don't accept the diaconate; many pastors will not cooperate with the deacons. Many of the faithful don't know what to do with the deacon's wife."[16] It is an interesting comparative fact of the present study that the deacons and their wives find a warmer welcome from the parishioners than from the priests. Only a small minority (16%) of deacons' wives feel that the parishioners are critical of them. On the other hand, they modestly disagree (65%) with the suggestion that deacons' wives "should enjoy special status in the parish." A peculiar observation is made by some women who say that they tend to "lose their identity and their name," and become known only as the deacon's wife. They sense a new and different perception. "People who were my friends now act as if I am a completely different person."

Through the experience of the formation program and the association with a diaconal husband, the wife is almost certain to become a "changed woman." From the perspective of social status, Marie Garon tells us that "it is easy to overlook the subtle but real manner in which a deacon's wife undergoes a change in life-style. Even though she does not obligate herself to any new or different activities, she experiences a change in attitude towards her on the part of parishioners, priests and religious."[17]

Nevertheless, in becoming known parochially as the deacon's wife, she is often sought out for advice and consultation. "People think I should have the answer for everything." This is not always a complaint. One wife observed: "I get the friendship and respect of our parishioners." Another appreciates the fact that "people will come to me and talk about God and ask for help in their problems. I feel that I am in a position to guide them in the direction to meet their needs." There is no question that those who have gone through the same training as their husbands are often competent to give spiritual guidance to others.

Widowers and Widows

The role of married deacon is logically attractive to men who had once aspired to the priesthood and had left the seminary. There is ample evidence that the greatest hindrance to the pursuit of the priestly vocation—and the main reason for dropping out of the seminary—is the requirement of celibacy. The restoration of the permanent diaconate has opened the possibility for the male Catholic to be both a clergyman and a married man. The first draft of the revised Code of Canon Law put no conditions on the matrimonial status of the deacon, but "at the eleventh hour" the Pope added a kind of "delayed celibacy" for deacons.

The duly ordained permanent deacon is not permitted to remarry if his wife dies, a prohibition that supposedly has an "ecumenical dimension," in the fact that the Eastern Uniate rites impose the same condition against clerical remarriage. The *Guidelines* (113) point out that "the Code of Canon Law preserves the traditional discipline of the Church; whereby, a married deacon who has been widowed may not enter a new marriage." The wives who want their husbands to be ordained, and who experience the several years of diaconal training, have no alternative but to abide by this prohibition. It is, however, the only aspect of the program to which the wives are almost unanimously opposed. Only ten percent of the respondents express themselves in favor of the prohibition of their husband's remarriage.

Exemptions from this prohibition can be obtained only from the Holy See, but the diocesan bishop says he is quite willing to apply for the rescript in the event of a wife's death. The most obvious reason for a dispensation is for the sake of young children who need the care of a mother. The prospect of motherless children is a strong motive why some women object to their husbands becoming deacons. A second strong reason is that the widowed deacon who has followed the vocation of sacramental marriage over the years is now deprived of this sacred state of life. Also, as one deacon observed: "It is a sobering thought to contemplate a life alone every night, after one has been happily married." To deny him this option seems to imply that marriage, although a sacrament, is somehow spiritually inferior to non-sacramental celibacy.

The demographic fact that women generally outlive men is true, of course, in this diocese, but there are only five widowers among the 150 deacons. In a sense, the diocese is experiencing an "aging diaconate," just as it has an aging priesthood. The average age of the deacons at this study is 57.3 years, of whom one-fifth are over seventy years of age. The oldest deacon reports that he was sixty-five when he applied for the first ordination Class of 1974. Several other deacons from the original class are also now well beyond the conventional age of retirement, but the bishop has not suggested that deacons be guided by the established retirement age for priests.

The problem of inevitable aging anticipates also the problems arising from illness or accidents. Permanent deacons in this diocese are required to carry insurance policies at their own expense. One of the wives pointed out that "the Church assumes no responsibility for an ill deacon or for the children of a deceased deacon." The typical deacon receives no stipend, or "stole fees," and is expected to be financially self-sufficient. Nevertheless, four out of ten (39%) of the deacons' wives think that "deacons should receive a salary for their work." What seems significant—and probably expected—is that the older wives are much more ready (55%) than the younger wives (23%) to say that their husbands should be salaried.

While not suggesting a salary, the Code of Canon Law anticipates health problems and decrees that clerics should receive "assistance by which their needs are suitably provided for, if they suffer from illness, incapacity or old age." (CIC 218, 2) The serious application of this canon has not yet been required in this diocese, but it is sure to become a matter of critical notice in the not too distant future. It may be said in general that "the issue of financial liability for permanent deacons is yet to be fully resolved."

What happens if the husband dies before his wife? The Church now has no experience with the widows of its married clergy. Does she just simply "drop out of sight"? The *Guidelines* for the diaconate (113) anticipates this question, with the advice that "widows of permanent deacons should be given sympathetic understanding by the local Church." There has been no discussion about a formal ministry to the widows of deacons at the present time, although it is clear that the Church of Apostolic times made careful provisions for widows. In his first letter to Timothy, Paul expresses concern for widows and recommends the kind of widow who has a "reputation for good deeds, a woman who brought up her children well, received strangers in her home, washed the feet of God's people, helped those in trouble, and gave herself to all kinds of good works." (I Tim. 5:9) It may be added that in later centuries, "widows appear to have played a more important role than deaconesses."[18]

Diaconal Community

One final diaconal prospect is in the sociological ideal of community among the deacons as individuals and among their wives as clergy couples. The sacrament of holy orders brings a man into the *ordo*, or body, of ordained ministers. This "fraternity" of the ordained clergy must be broadened to the concept of community by including the wives, but must be narrowed by the unwillingness of priests to be associated closely with deacons. A communal element is essential "to the exercise of ordained ministry," but it appears to be a male element in the statement that "the mutual support and *fraternity* of deacons are not just sociological or psychological useful things; they are integral parts of the meaning of their vocation." (124 *Guidelines*)

If the formation of a diaconal community results from the fact of ordination, membership has to exclude women who are never ordained. Among the diaconal couples, however, the sense of community evolves from close association during the formation program and is a kind of "class" loyalty. As Marie Garon reflects, "during the three years that our husbands were in training for the permanent diaconate, a strong sense of community developed among the couples."[19] After ordination the ministry called them to different locations and to separate ways. It required special initiative to establish and maintain an ongoing "support group" of deacons' wives in this diocese, in which there was much more participation by the younger wives (46%) than by the older women (10%).

If there is a sense of fraternity among the diocesan priests, it usually centers around "classmates" who shared their seminary experiences up to ordination. Close, lifelong friendships are sometimes maintained among these men. The diaconate program is still too young to reveal this kind of camaraderie among "classmates." Incorporating the wives into their ordination, class community is weakened by several factors, mainly because less than half of the wives (41%) report that they attended "all" or "almost all" of the training classes. The proportion who attended classes with their husbands shifted drastically over the years. In the earliest ordination classes only 16% attended that frequently, while this proportion grew to 49% in the most recent classes.

If the permanent deacons were a "cross-cut" of the diocesan People of God, and if the diocese itself were a Christian fellowship of love and justice and equality, one could speak seriously of a diaconal Christian community. Ethnic and racial diversity hinders the development of community. Out of an expanding population of Catholic Hispanics, only four Hispanic deacons were ordained. Out of over 90,000 Afro-American Catholics in the diocese, only thirteen are permanent deacons. Two out of five (42%) of the wives agree that the diocese should ordain more Black deacons; only six percent disagree, and the rest are "neutral." Social status differs by education and occupation. Practically all deacons ordained in the last ten years have at least a high-school education and at least eight out of ten now have some college experience. Since the married deacon has to support his family, the pool of prospective candidates tends to be limited to professionals and white-collar workers with a steady income.

There is no question that the permanent deacons and their wives are a "select" group of Christians. We know that scores of Catholic couples come forward every two years when the "call" is advertised for candidates. We must assume that about two-thirds of the couples who apply do not have an authentic vocation for the diaconal ministry because they are turned away, "de-selected," from the formation program. Racial, ethnic and class distinctions exist in the Catholic population and it is no surprise that they are reflected also among the permanent deacons.

Endnotes

1. Aime' Georges Martimort, *Deaconesses: An Historical Study,* San Francisco, Ignatius Press, 1986, pp. 148-150.

2. Joan Morris, *The Lady Was a Bishop,* New York, Macmillan, 1973, p. 76.

3. *New Woman—New Church—New Priestly Ministry,* Maureen Dwyer, ed., Proceedings of Second WOC Conference, Rochester, Kirk-Wood, 1980, p. 176.

4. *Partners in the Mystery of Redemption, Origins,* vol. 18, April 21, 1988, para. 219.

5. *Permanent Deacons in the United States: Guidelines on their Formation and Ministry,* Washington, United States Catholic Conference, 1985 (Revision of 1971 Guidelines).

6. For other "Issues in the Diaconate," see Dean Hoge, *Future of Catholic Leadership,* Kansas City, Sheed & Ward, 1987, pp. 194-197.

7. This sentiment is reflected by Ernest J. Fiedler, "Permanent Deacons Shouldn't Play Priest," *U. S. Catholic*, May, 1986, pp. 15-16.

8. See Tim McCarthy, "Deacons: To Be, or What To Be," *National Catholic Reporter*, March 15, 1985, pp. 15, 26-27.

9. "Married deacons represent a past, temporary accommodation with a clerically dominated Church. As such, they are anachronistic." Eugene Kennedy, *The Now and Future Church*, Garden City, Doubleday, 1984, p. 171.

10. "Partners," para. 122.

11. *One in Christ Jesus, Origins*, vol. 20, April 5, 1990, para. 120.

12. "Partners," para. 244.

13. *A National Survey of the Permanent Diaconate in the United States*, Washington, U. S. Catholic Conference, 1981, p.41.

14. *One in Christ Jesus*, para. 5.

15. *Ibid.*, para. 123.

16. Leonard Doohan, "Ministry and Spirituality for Deacons and their wives," *Diaconate Magazine*, January/February, 1986, pp. 15-19.

17. Marie R. Garon, "New Role for Women—Deacon's Wife," *Diaconate Magazine*, September/October, 1985, pp. 9-11.

18. Martimort, *op. cit.*, p. 5.

19. Marie R. Garon, "Wife-Support Equals Life-Support," *Deacon Digest*, November, 1984, pp. 17, 22.

Chapter Six

Wives of Convert Priests

Cornelia Connelly was the wife of the Episcopal rector of Trinity Church in Natchez, Mississippi. In 1835 she and her husband converted to the Catholic Church and lived as devout lay persons, until Pierce Connelly petitioned the Vatican for acceptance to the Roman priesthood. There were no "Pastoral Provisions" in those days for married Catholic clergy. The marriage had to break up by a Vatican divorce. In March, 1844, a papal decree of "permanent separation" was granted to them. In the following year, when Pierce was ordained a Catholic priest, Cornelia was admitted to the Convent of the Sacred Heart. As Cardinal Wiseman pointed out, "The Church never sanctions a married man to be a priest without his wife at least taking a vow of chastity, but I think I can say never without her embracing the religious state."[1] Cornelia remained steadfast to her vows in the religious sisterhood, but he apostatized later and instituted proceedings in the Anglican ecclesiastical court, "to claim restitution of conjugal rights and force his wife to return to him."[2]

For many centuries the Church had forbidden marriage to its ordained clergy, a prohibition that was hesitantly lifted with the permission of Pope Pius XII. He granted an indulgence to Bishop Alberto Stohr, of Mainz, Germany, in favor of Rudolf Goethe, a married Lutheran pastor who was ordained a Catholic priest on his seventy-first birthday in 1951. In the following year, two younger Lutheran ministers, Eugen Scheytt and Otto Melchers, also made the transfer. Then, in December, 1953, Martin Giebner became the fourth married convert to minister as a Catholic priest in Germany. None of these priests was forced to relinquish marital relations with his spouse.[3]

There is apparently no historical or ecclesiastical reason why the post-war German hierarchy felt free to make these requests of the Holy See. So-called "liberal" prelates, like Cardinal Cushing of Boston and Cardinal Ritter of St. Louis, are known to have turned down such requests. In the next decade, several Americans, who were rejected by bishops in this country, turned to Germany for help. Ernest Beck, a married Lutheran minister, was advised by Monsignor Hellriegel to seek ordination from the Archbishop of Mainz in 1964. Another appeal to German episcopal influence was made in 1966 by Father Louis Sigman, who got the intervention of Abbot Lorenz Klein, at the Benedictine Abbey of Trier, Germany. He proved that his Episcopal ordaining prelate had been consecrated by a Polish Catholic Bishop who in turn had been consecrated by the Archbishop of Utrecht. Asked if he was willing to accept ordination *sub condicione,* he was the first to be ordained conditionally by an American Bishop, John Franz, of Peoria.[4]

The question of a married clergy was not discussed at the Second Vatican Council, but near the end of the Council, Pope Paul VI promised the Council Fathers that he intended "to give new luster and strength to priestly celibacy in the world of today." This promise was kept in his encyclical, *Sacerdotalis Coelibatus,* in 1967. In the middle of this letter, and almost unexpectedly, he suggested that, "a study may be allowed of the particular circumstances of married sacred ministers of Churches, or other Christian communities separated from the Catholic Communion, and of the possibility of admitting to priestly functions those who desire to adhere to the fullness of this Communion and to continue to exercise the sacred ministry." He was careful to add that, "the circumstances must be such, however, as not to prejudice the existing discipline regarding celibacy."[5]

The American Experience

It was not until 1980 that the Holy See granted permission to the American hierarchy to accept married Episcopal clergy to the Catholic priesthood. Under the so-called "Pastoral Provisions," the Vatican no longer demands that the couple be divorced and dedicated to a life of celibacy when the married Episcopal priest is ordained to the Catholic priesthood. Unlike Cornelia Connelly, the wife is not required to spend the rest of her life in a convent. But there is no official protocol to guide her into the new and untried role of wife to a Roman Catholic priest. How does she react to this "strange" situation? Is she accepted in the spirit of Christian love by clergy and laity, or is she simply dismissed as the "priest's woman," as she is dubbed by some envious celibate clergy? By means of interviews and questionnaires we have arrived at some explanatory sociological generalizations.

Roman Catholic priests who are married under the Pastoral Provisions represent a minuscule percentage of the U. S. Catholic clergy, which means also that their wives are few in number—less than four dozen all told. It must be noted that these women did not enter into marriage with Catholic priests. They were already married to Anglican clergymen who then brought them along upon conversion to the Catholic faith and ordination to the Catholic priesthood. The forty-fourth married convert priest, Trevor Nicholls, was ordained by Cardinal O'Connor in January, 1990. This exemplifies the unusual situation where the Catholic Church ordains men who are already married (but does not marry men who are already ordained).

This arrangement is such a novelty in the U. S. Catholic Church that it raises large questions in the minds of traditional Catholics: why are some priests permitted to have wives while the great majority must remain celibate? Why are not the wives of resigned Catholic priests invited to share the same status enjoyed by the wives of former Episcopalian clergy? The answer to this riddle and the definition of the authentic wife of the Catholic priest lies in the correct interpretation of the Pastoral Provisions.

The process for their acceptance began in 1977 when a handful of Episcopal clergy—with no inducement from the Catholic hierarchy—applied to the Holy See for admission to the priesthood of the Church of Rome. They requested that they could continue their priestly ministry in the Catholic Church without divorcing their wives or refraining from marital relations, as had been the ancient prohibition. Their request was submitted to Rome by the U. S. National Conference of Catholic Bishops and was answered affirmatively in June, 1980, by Cardinal Franjo Seper, Prefect of the Sacred Congregation for the Defense of the Faith.[6]

The Vatican seemed to have some misgivings about this sexually-liberating procedure when its document stated that, "with regard to the Church's traditional discipline of celibacy for her priestly ministers, it must be ensured that there be no scandal, that priests and people understand this exception to the traditional discipline." In other words, the general rule of clergy celibacy was not to be relaxed, but the exceptions were to be handled with the utmost caution. To avoid a further possibility of scandal to the faithful, the married priest should be assigned to administrative or educational tasks and kept away from the parochial pastoral ministry (cura animarum).

The program got its serious start in March, 1981, when Bishop Bernard Law, of Springfield, Missouri, was delegated by Rome to take charge of the procedures. Under his guidance, the Reverend Luther Parker, who was sponsored by Bishop Ernest Unterkoefler for the Diocese of Charleston, took instructions to become a Catholic, and in June, 1982, was the first of the married priests to be ordained under the provisions.[7] It is expected, of course, but not mandatory, that the priest's wife follow him into the Catholic Church. Thus, it happened that Mary Alma Parker became the first "priest's wife" under the new dispensation and a "pioneer" among American Catholic women. She already had twenty-five years' experience as a clergyman's wife before she shifted her faith affiliation, but there were no Catholic models for her to follow.

Vital Statistics

The number of priests' wives coming into the Church is relatively small and we were able to reach almost all of them, as well as their priest-husbands. While all are "new" to the life of a Catholic priest's spouse, they vary in the length of years they had spent as homemaker in the Anglican parsonage. Three out of ten had been the Episcopal priest's wife for less than ten years, while in the older category one-quarter had been in married life for more than twenty years. On the average, they had spent 16.2 years in their clerical marriage. Their ages range from the youngest at 32 years to the oldest at 61, with the average age at 42.9 years. There is a range also in the amount of education; they average 14.8 years of schooling. One-quarter had earned graduate degrees, while one quarter did not attend college at all. The extent of their education may be relative to the time of life when they married. One in four married before the husband entered seminary, one in three while he was a seminary student—where the wife took some part-time courses—and the remaining marriages occurred after seminary graduation and ordination.[8]

While all of the wives were devout Episcopalians at the time when they converted to Catholicism, less than half had been "cradle" Episcopalians. The others, in order of frequency, had been Roman Catholics and Methodists, with a scattering of Baptists, Brethren, Lutherans, and Presbyterians. In other words, more than half had changed religion twice since childhood.[9] One lone holdout said, "I switched from Baptist to Methodist for him, and from Methodist to Episcopalian with him. I'm not changing again." While none of them said she herself has a vocation to the ordained priesthood, almost half the respondents think their marriage to a priest is a "special" kind of religious or Church calling.

None of these respondents is childless. Those who are still in the child-bearing years have an average of 3.3 children apiece, while the older wives who have "completed" their families have an average of four children. With few exceptions, the children have followed their parents into the Catholic Church and, in most cases, those of elementary school age are enrolled at the local parochial school. The great majority like to think of themselves as simply "wife and homemaker," but during the course of their married life two-thirds of them have been gainfully employed outside the home.

Break with the Past

Giving up one's faith commitment to join another Church—even when both religions are as similar as Anglicanism and Catholicism—has to be an emotionally tense experience. The Episcopal Church no longer "deposes" the resigned priest and, in about half the cases, the Episcopal Bishops were both cooperative and cordial. Several, however, were downright hostile and "were glad to get rid of us." One-third of the women said that the shift from the Episcopal Church temporarily alienated them from their family and relatives. Almost all of them, however, still maintain good personal relations with former friends and associates.

Much has been made of the hardship and financial deprivation suffered by the clerical couple while switching to the Catholic faith. Father John Jay Hughes says their sacrifices "are heroic," because "overnight the clergyman passes from being a respected figure in the community, with a comfortable home, good income and near total security, to homelessness, unemployment, food stamps, utility cutoffs, even welfare."[10] Most of the wives thought that this experience was "tolerable" or "not so bad," while the remaining minority report it as a "severe hardship."

One wife said that her father, a successful businessman, gave her husband a friendly warning: "I have nothing against the Catholics," he said, "but you are now making twice as much as you'll ever make as a Catholic priest." None of the wives anticipated large financial rewards in the Catholic ministry but, in comparison with their previous economic status, six out of ten say that their current social status is lower. The same proportion reside in a house of their own (but with a mortgage still to be paid off). For the most part, they are uncertain what benefits will accrue to wife and children from the diocesan priests' pension program.

The wives were willing to spell out their attitudes on some of the pertinent ecclesiastical matters. Perhaps an unexpected opinion is that only one-third of them were ready to say that diocesan priests should be allowed optional celibacy. "After all," said one almost apologetically, "we are supposed to accept what the Pope teaches." Most of them are also sure that the Holy Father will never permit the priestly ordination of women. Only one out of six is "feminist" enough to insist on the use of "inclusive" language in the liturgy. One of the more "delicate" questions we asked concerns the establishment of "Anglican-use" congregations. The majority responded unfavorably, but several said that the Church should "allow" rather than "encourage" these units of common identity.[11]

Taking Instructions

Since all of the priests' wives had been raised in the Christian religion, their willingness to accept the teachings of the Catholic Church did not require a major shift of beliefs. For the most part, they were not called upon to follow the usual course of "convert instructions" for persons seeking baptism. With their husbands, they received the sacrament of Confirmation, but in contrast to the rigorous academic examinations to which their husbands submitted, they were not subject to doctrinal examination. The majority said they had informal conversations, rather than formal "catechesis," with the Catholic priest designated as mentor for their husband. The time required in preparation for the Profession of Faith which incorporated them into the Catholic Church was relatively short, in most instances only a few months.

After their admission to the Church, the applicants, both husband and wife, were expected to live as lay parishioners for one year before the ordination of the husband. In the testimony of the wives, however, this period of waiting ranged from one year in some instances to more than three years in others. Strictly speaking, this delay was irrelevant to the wife's readiness for her new role. It was her husband's "papers" that had to be cleared by the Vatican. More than half of the wives judged their waiting period to be "too lengthy," while one-third thought it to be "about right," and a few said it was "quicker than expected."

The length of time in this waiting period is due in part to the effort involved in assembling a dossier of thirteen required documents. The priest's wife is the object of some of this enquiry. A copy of the marriage record must be provided, as well as "evidence of the stability and health of the marriage satisfactory to the sponsoring Ordinary." The individual who supplies this testimony should not be a lay person, a friend or relative, or even a religious Sister or Brother. The assurance of marital stability has to come from a clergyman, preferably the local priest who had been appointed by the bishop as mentor to the candidate.

This mentor comes to know the clergy couple better than anyone else in the diocese and probably has to give counsel to the wife about the unknown role of a Catholic priest's wife. Like her husband, she usually makes the Profession of Faith, but is not required to sign a document to that effect. With her husband she usually submits to psychiatric evaluation through the Minnesota Multiphasic Personality Inventory, at the hands of an appointed psychologist. She is required also to sign a statement "advising of her agreement to, and support of, her husband's petition for priesthood in the Catholic Church." If there are minor children, it is the wife and mother who assures that they will receive Catholic schooling.

One interesting omission from the official dossier is any mention of vocational priority. Unlike the careful instructions given to diaconate candidates, for whom developmental programs are necessary, the married priest is not told that "commitment to wife and family has clear priority over ministry."[12] The wives to whom I put this question did not hesitate to say that the duties of the priesthood had to have clear priority over anything else.[13] Occasionally, a wife remarks that her priest-husband spends hours out of the house nights and weekends, but she does not complain that this is a detriment to their marriage and family.

The majority of wives found the interim period a kind of "limbo" that was fraught with tension, uncertainty and apprehension. At this point, her future did not depend upon herself. It was tied to the negotiations through which her husband was gaining the rescript for ordination. The approval had to come from Rome, but once it was obtained, setting the actual date of ordination was the prerogative of the diocesan bishop, who in most instances took little interest in the wife's preparedness for her new role. We asked whether the wives were tested, examined or interviewed by the bishop or his delegates. More than two-thirds replied that their contact with the bishop was at best through informal conversation. Only one out of four reported in-depth interviews or psychological testing.

Once they have settled into their diocesan assignment, the wives continue to learn about life among the Catholics. We asked whether they experienced any resentment or unfriendliness among the laity. "We still live in the same house," reports one lady, "and the Catholic neighbors now welcome us to the parish church. They could not be more kind to us." The majority report a friendly acceptance by the laity, but in a few instances they were treated coldly by deacons' wives and by Irish-born clergy. More than one of the respondents feel that "some celibate priests tend to be envious" of them.

Role Preparation

The careful preparation and retraining of the convert priest-husbands were not duplicated for their wives. No diocese offers to provide preparatory training for their novel role. As one lady said, "there is no one to give us such training." There are no role models for the Catholic priest's wife, no bishops' wives from whom she could "learn the ropes."[14] There is no guidance in Canon Law, or in the books on Applied Theology, or in the many surveys that have been made of the Catholic parish ministry. One of the younger women was asked by her bishop how she was going to act as a priest's wife when there is nobody to imitate. She replied, "that ought to be wonderful because there is nothing for the people to expect. Whatever I do will be the way the wife of a priest is supposed to behave."[15]

One critical difference for the wife of the Catholic priest is that her husband will no longer center his ministry on the parish. One of the pastoral provisions says that the convert priest may not be assigned to a primary *cura animarum*, or direct pastoral ministry. He is not to be the typical parish priest, which was his main experience during the years in an Episcopal parish. The bishops are constrained from this appointment at the very place where the shortage of priests is most serious. The bishop tends to appoint the convert married priest as associate (not in residence) for a particular parish. In most cases he celebrates a daily Mass in the parish church, as well as a Saturday evening Mass and one on Sunday. He is generally available for infant baptisms, confessions, funerals, wakes, weddings, and sick calls. Although this variety of part-time work encompasses the full round of tasks required normally of parish priests, the appointments are euphemistically termed a "secondary" ministry.

For the priest's wife there are two important differences in this arrangement. She does not live in a parsonage, as in the Episcopal parish, and is thus physically removed from the everyday life of the local church members. The typical survey response is that, "I now feel less part of his ministry than I did." One of the wives remarked: "I have much less to do, many fewer Church obligations than I had in the Episcopal Church. On the other hand, my husband is much busier than he ever was." The other difference is that her husband usually has a full-time, income-producing, non-parochial occupation. He may be a high-school or college teacher, a campus minister, a chaplain in a hospital or prison, assistant in the Chancery office, or administrator in some diocesan institution.

Often enough in these official appointments the married priest goes to work in the morning, returns in the evening like any other employed head of household. He is sometimes absent from the home doing "priestly work" evenings and weekends at the very time when most men are able to be with their family.

This obviously means, as the wives say, "My husband now has less time for the family." The wife is not likely to have any direct participation in her husband's regular workday. Among the younger women her energies are centered on the home, keeping house and garden, raising children. The reason why many of the wives are employed outside the home is not solely to obtain more income; it gives them "something to do."

Her home is not the typical parish rectory, and in most instances, it is not even in the territorial parish where her husband serves as associate priest. It is their parish of residence (not in her husband's parish) where she may belong to the Mothers' Club, the Altar Guild, or any other conventional parish group. This fixed residence decreases the likelihood that the bishop will change assignments, as is the case with the celibate diocesan priests who have to be ready to accept a different assignment on short notice.

Thinking with the Church

There can be no question about the "orthodoxy" in belief and practice among these wives of Catholic priests. They had no hesitancy in making the Profession of Faith in accepting the complete credo of Catholicism. We went beyond the conventional catechetical boundaries by enquiring about their acceptance of pastoral letters and other public statements of the NCCB. The wives are, of course, unanimous in their promotion of the Pro-Life Movement. They are not quite so ready to underwrite the bishops' dislike of ERA. In fact, one-third of the wives express approval of the women's Equal Rights Amendment.

We asked whether they thought that the pastoral provision couples are social and political conservatives. Two-thirds of them think so, but they are quick to add that, "this is just a guess because we hardly know them." In fact, the survey responses show that they share some of the "liberal" attitudes of the hierarchy. Four social issues, promoted by the NCCB, are supported by the majority of spouses: They oppose capital punishment, and are in favor of low-cost housing, civil rights of minorities, and legislation for handgun control.

On the other hand, some of the issues favored by the NCCB find varying degrees of disfavor among the wives. They are unwilling to support the annual guaranteed family wage and the bishops' opposition to nuclear deterrence. They do not favor higher social welfare payments, unionization of migrant farm workers, or the defense of illegal alien immigrants. On some of these items they declare themselves "neutral" rather than in opposition. These responses, however, do not support the contention of some Catholic "liberals," that these converts will impede the Church's teachings on social justice.

Partners in Ministry

In what sense are these women entering a new and strange kind of life when they embark upon the role of spouse to a Catholic priest? Unlike the wives of most Protestant clergy, they had no formal expectations for church ministry in the Episcopal parsonage. Most of them, however, had previously taken an active part in the life of the Episcopalian parish. They also said that they had frequently entertained parishioners in the parsonage and had many close friends among them. In their current role they have yet to develop a circle of close Catholic women friends. The majority do not consider themselves a "partner" in their husband's priesthood. At the same time, they say that there are now "fewer church demands" made on them. There are reasons to think that they are now even further from the heart of their husband's sacerdotal ministry.

When we asked if their husband works harder now than he did as an Episcopal priest, their answer is ambivalent in the sense that he has been a hard worker in both situations. Most of them deny that their husband now has "less time for the family." The comparisons may not be clear-cut because in most instances, the husband now has a different set of tasks. In the Episcopal Church, practically all of them had been parish priests. Except for the few who are in an "Anglican-use" congre-

gation, the priests are in non-parochial activities like administration, chaplaincies and teaching.[4]

These wives are now dedicated and devout Catholics, whose
"church work" is that of the active parishioner. Their residence,
in well over half of the cases, is not in the parish where their
husbands are called on for "week-end supply." The pressing
problem of the priest shortage creates many opportunities for
priestly ministry at the parish level, even though the provisions
forbid a full-time parochial assignment.

Units of Common Identity

It may be too soon to make a judgment about the continued
existence of the "Anglican-usage" congregations, which were introduced by a special provision of the 1980 Vatican agreement
to accept married Episcopal Priests. One of the pastors, Father
Clark Tea, of the Church of the Virgin, in Las Vegas, is a celibate priest. The others are married men and they are the only
priest-converts who are officially assigned to a parish. As we
have seen, the ruling from Rome is that the convert priests
were not to be assigned to the care of parishioners in the numerous Latin-rite parishes.

These parishes turn out to be a minority within the minority
of the clergy couples we have been discussing. These few wives
are different because they have not been required to relinquish
their status as lady of the parsonage. They were not forced to
make the relatively abrupt role change that the other wives experienced. They continue to be the parson's wife dealing with
parishioners just as they had been doing in the Episcopal parish. Their conversion to Catholicism and the Profession of Faith
were shared by all the lay members of the community. As one
wife remarked, "we are happier and more adjusted religiously
than we were as Episcopalians."

The Anglican-usage communities are much smaller than the
average Roman Catholic parish, but are of a size similar to the
average Episcopal Church parish. Basically, there is no real ad-

justment to be made in dealing with the parishioners. "They seem to think and act like the Episcopal lay people we have always known. Although, like us, they are now Roman Catholics, they do not seem to behave any differently from Anglican parishioners. Like us, they have made the formal break from our previous Church, and in this sense we do share an important similar conversion and faith commitment."

While the priest's wife shares a parochial solidarity with the lay people, she feels isolated from the other wives in Anglican-use parishes. They are in widely separated dioceses and their husbands went to different seminaries. Except by letter and telephone, they meet once a year under the auspices of the Association of Anglican-use congregations, promoted by its president, Father Clark Tea. They have to feel strange and separate from the other Catholic parishes in their city simply because they are looked upon as a "semi-Protestant" oddity in the diocese: "Catholic women tend to be friendly when we meet, but there is not the warmth we once knew in parish life."

This handful of clergy wives is even more isolated than the other provisional couples. There is no special relationship with the Catholic bishop as there had been with the Episcopal bishop. The wives' support group they had previously enjoyed is now a happy memory. In a sense, these are the "strangest" of the priests' wives and the least likely to be accepted with warmth and friendship by other Catholic women. One may speculate whether these kinds of church congregations are going to continue.

Mutual Support

One final note may be made about the relative "isolation" of these Catholic clergy couples: Most of them are in a geographical area other than the location where they had been active in the Episcopal Church. They are also, for the most part, distant from other "pastoral provision" couples. In answer to our question about mutual support groups, the majority of wives said they favor some form of contact with the others. In recalling the

Danvers Conference meeting in 1984, which the more recent converts did not attend, the majority are in favor of an occasional group conference.

One of the supportive characteristics for these wives when they were in the Episcopal Church was the network of wives with whom they could associate.[16] As one convert priest says about the Catholic Church, "there are no clergy wives gatherings, obviously. We laugh when we say that, but that was a significant part of ministry in the Episcopal Church—the wives played a big role—there was a close sense of fraternity, not only among the Episcopal priests, but among their families." Three or four times a year they gathered somewhere in the diocese for a meeting, a luncheon, or Kafee Klatch and discussion. This was the informal support group, in which they exchanged experiences, frustrations and aspirations. Shared prayer was an integral part of this mutual support.

The great majority of respondents to this wives' survey were eager and affirmative to the suggestion that there should be "some type of informal contact among the pastoral provision couples." They expressed themselves almost unanimously in favor of "an occasional conference of clergy couples similar to the meeting at Danvers, in November, 1984." They are also personally willing to cooperate in the production and distribution of an intermittent newsletter for married clergy couples. This desire for mutual support and contact is reflected in the words of one priest who remarked, "It's a lot harder being the wife of a priest when there is no contact with other wives like that. It's even more difficult now because we don't really know what to expect."

Some of the wives had anticipated a continuing informal relationship with the pastoral provision "office," under the auspices of Father Luther Parker, who had provided guidance and support in the early days of the transfer process. Once their husbands are ordained and settled in their new diocese, the wives feel that they have been "dropped" by Cardinal Law's surrogate. "I had not expected that we would be so quickly on our own," as one wife observed. It is almost as though the married clergy couples are expected to ignore, or forget, that they are unique among the celibate priesthood. It is probably too soon to expect that they can be fully assimilated in the Catholic population.

On the other hand, the wives of Catholic priests are so few in number and so widely scattered around the country, that they do not have access to anything like a wives' support group. One may talk cheerfully about Catholic community and solidarity, the mystical Body of Christ, in which all Christians are united. In this perspective, the priest's wife may simply be absorbed into the parish community like all other parishioners; but the fact is that she is not just another parishioner. Catholics—including bishops and priests—don't quite know what to make of her and she herself is not quite sure how she fits into the world of Roman Catholicism.

One final question may ask whether the Catholic priest's wife really wants to replicate her earlier experiences as the Episcopal parson's wife. Few of them agree that they should make a "clean break" with the Episcopal past. In fact, some of them continue to maintain good personal relations with former Episcopal friends and associates. They express mixed feelings. Few of them have been alienated from their friends and relatives; none of them regrets having made the switch to Catholicism. They have fond remembrance of their Episcopalian past and a genuine love for Episcopalians. At the same time, they feel it is necessary to distance themselves from the past: "We are now completely Roman Catholic. There is no use in being nostalgic."

Endnotes

1. Juliana Wadham, *The Case of Cornelia Connelly*, London, Collins, 1956, p. 151.

2. Mother Marie Therese, *Cornelia Connelly: A Study in Fidelity*, London, Burns & Oates, 1963, p. 100.

3. Rudolf Goethe, "Die Offene Tur," pp. 117-165, in *Bekenntnis zur Katholishe Kirche*, Wurzburg, 1955.

4. Joseph H. Fichter, *The Pastoral Provisions: Married Catholic Priests*, Kansas City, Sheed & Ward, 1989, p. 69.

5. Pope Paul VI, *Sacerdotalis Coelibatus*, June 24, 1967, art. 43.

6. First reported, "On File," in *Origins*, September 4, 1980, p. 178.

7. James Parker, "A Married Catholic Priest?" pp. 169-172, in Dan O'Neill, ed., *The New Catholics*, New York, Crossroad, 1987.

8. A contemporary Episcopalian survey found that at time of marriage, one-third of husbands were already priests; 28 percent were either deacons or seminarians. John and Linda Morgan, *Wives of Priests*, Notre Dame, Parish Life Institute, 1980, p. 12.

9. In the Morgan Study, 59% of the wives were converts to the Episcopal Church, *ibid.*, p. 12.

10. Quoted in Fichter, *Pastoral Provisions*, p. 67.

11. Joseph H. Fichter, "Parishes for Anglican-Usage," in *America*, 1987, pp. 354-357, reprinted in *Catholic Digest*, May, 1988, pp. 94-96.

12. *A National Study of the Permanent Diaconate*, Washington, United States Catholic Conference, 1981, p. 26.

13. When Pierce Connelly wanted to resume his marriage with Cornelia, he reverted to this priority: "I am a man, a husband, and a father before I am a priest, and my first duties cannot be abandoned." Juliana Wadham: *The Case of Cornelia Connelly*, London, Collins, 1956, p. 150.

14. This is in contrast to clergy wives in the Protestant Churches. See William Douglas, *Ministers' Wives*, New York, Harper & Row, 1965, pp. 168-169.

15. Joseph H. Fichter, "Wives of Catholic Priests," in *Church*, Spring, 1990, pp. 53-56.

16. See John and Linda Morgan, *op. cit.*, chap. 5, "Social and Ethical Life."

Chapter Seven

Wives of Resigned Priests

There was always a small number of American priests who had resigned their ministry and married "outside the Church," but little notice was ever taken of their wives. Unlike Katherine von Bora, who married ex-monk Martin Luther and became celebrated among the early reformers,[1] these wives slipped quietly into the tasks of everyday living, motherhood and family. In official Church language, before the Second Vatican Council, such marriages were "invalid"; the priest's wife was his "female accomplice," and both were automatically excommunicated. There were some, however, who did not go quietly and unobtrusively. The most noisy were the ex-priests who edited *The Converted Catholic Magazine*,[2] and who insisted that the rule of celibacy was equally erroneous as all other doctrines of the Catholic Church.

Occasionally a carefully reasoned explanation was published why the priest left his vocation and even the Church. Although the departure coincided with marriage, the love of the wife was not always presented as the reason for leaving.[3] On the other hand, wrote one departing priest, "I wanted the Archbishop to know that I was offering him my resignation for one reason only: I wanted to marry." He said he was reluctant to resign and he "was not resigning because of the priesthood, but because of celibacy."[4] This was the clearly expressed intention of the founders of the National Association for Pastoral Renewal, established by a group of St. Louis priests in 1967. It is also the continuing theme of non-canonical married priests and their wives, wherever they have organized in America and internationally.

Sporadic research efforts have been made, especially by psychologists, into the lives of resigned priests, mainly to search out their motivation. Comparisons of relatively small numbers of resigned priests with non-resigned priests looked for personality variables, emotional development, ego-strength, hypochondriasis. Two doctoral dissertations may be mentioned as examples of such research: R. W. Nichols compared 67 resigned priests with 46 non-resigned, and C. Noty compared 67 resigned with 63 non-resigned.[5] Neither claims to have used a random sample and did not focus on the wives of these priests.

No researcher has been able to obtain a satisfactory representative sample of the wives of American resigned priests, or even a reliable estimate of their numbers. A common estimate is that upward of 16,000 resigned priests now live in the United States, the great majority of them married. Partial lists of names of wives of priests are provided in two available directories: The National Association for a Married Priesthood published the CORPUS *Directory*, listing names of resigned priests, their wives and children.[6] Another source of wives' names is Martin J. Hegarty's WEORC *Employment Directory,* which, in its third edition of 1986 had more than 1,850 entries.[7] Maureen Hendricks' survey in 1979 dealt with a non-random sample of 460 resigned priests and 451 wives of resigned priests who volunteered to respond and who were contacted through organizations and religious orders, and through newspaper and magazine ads.[8]

Marital Stability

Among the numerous studies that have been made of resigned priests in the United States, Hendricks' is unique in focusing directly on the priests' wives. "Previous speculation about these marriages," she says, "tended to be pessimistic." Psychiatrist James Gill, in 1969, held out no hope for their marital happiness, observing that the priests who leave and marry are all depressed.[9] The Bishops' national survey, published in 1972, asked no questions of priests' wives, but found that the married resignees were fairly happy, even at the expense of some tension.[10]

Hendricks observes that, "the loneliness which mandatory celibacy engenders has been well-studied and documented as a significant factor in the resignation of priests." Previous studies paid attention to the resigned priest but "failed to ask what the wives thought of the marriages. Since the women are 50 percent of these married-priest couples, a valid picture of such marriages needs to include background data on the women, as well as their evaluation of the marriages."[11] She asked about "courtship" patterns and found that 87% of the wives had met their husbands while the priests were still officially within the structure. It is of interest that 73% of the wives first dated their husbands while they were still in the priesthood. Also, 37 percent of them became engaged while he was still in the active ministry. The priests were asked: "How long did you go with your wife?" The average length of time was 18.5 months, ranging from one month to ten years and three months.[12]

Other pertinent findings included that, "the men were more likely to view themselves as priests than were their wives. More resigned nun-wives viewed their husbands as priests than any of the other women." Again, "about 67% of the resigned married priests still see themselves as priests, while 20% would not return to work as a priest. Almost 33% still celebrate Mass; less than 5% 'never' attend Mass." In summary: "Approximately 87% of the wives had met their husbands while the men were still in the active priesthood; 73% first dated their future husbands then, but only 37% became engaged."[13]

"The education of the women in the study was more advanced than women in the general population and only 34% were not employed outside the home. An important bias in the study was the fact that approximately 56% of the subjects belonged to an association [CORPUS] specifically dedicated to obtaining functional status within the Roman Catholic Church for resigned married priests." Furthermore, "there is evidence that couples in which the wife was a resigned nun had greater marital satisfaction than other resigned priest-married couples. The marriage partners were found to have significantly greater marital happiness than marriage partners in the general population."[14]

New Beginnings

At the very time when Hendricks was gathering the data for her excellent survey, negotiations were under way to make room for married priests in the Catholic Church. While many of the resigned priests continued to lobby for optional celibacy and for the recognition of their own marital status, Cardinal Franjo Seper was entertaining applications from American married clergy of the Episcopal Church who wanted to switch to the Church of Rome.[15] The fact that Rome cooperated with these petitions opened a flood of protests over the so-called "double standard." The program for pastoral provisions is still in its formative stages and is considered merely "experimental" by many observers.

Although the Holy See eventually made "provisions" for the acceptance of converted married priests of other Christian denominations, it has not made similar concessions for resigned priests who have married. "The explanation why the Episcopal priest may bring his wife with him and why the resigned Catholic priest may not has been put in the 'bluntest' moral terms. The man who abandons the Episcopal Church to join the true Church of Rome is to be praised for good moral behavior. He deserves commendations and rewards. The man who abandons the Catholic priesthood to take a wife is to be blamed for reprehensible moral behavior. He is to be scolded and penalized. In the former case, it does not matter that the priest is married; in the latter case, it is the only thing that matters. In the first case, he has to leave his Church but retains his wife; in the second, he has to leave his wife to retain his Church."[16]

When the Holy See grants a dispensation from clerical celibacy, "the rescript embraces inseparably the return to the lay state and dispensation from the obligations arising from Sacred Orders. Never is the petitioner permitted to separate these two elements, or to accept the one and refuse the other."[17] In other words, the priest who is now allowed to marry must be simultaneously "reduced" to the status of the laity and relieved of all duties and privileges associated with the priesthood. A significant number object strenuously to this condition, claiming that holy orders can never be erased from a priest. Many do not even apply for the dispensation to marry if they have to stop being priests. One wife said, "the Bishop offered to help regularize our marriage with an appeal to the Holy Father, but my husband refused his offer. He insists that his resignation was from celibacy, not from priesthood."

Since the death of Pope Paul VI, the Vatican officials seem to have become much more negative toward the resigned priests. The reigning Pontiff, John Paul II, has practically closed down the process of dispensations from the vow of celibacy. A survey, conducted by the Canon Law Society of America in 1983, found that Cardinal Ratzinger's guidelines "allow a priest to be laicized only if he was patently not ready/suitable at the time of ordination, or if he has been away from ministry for a long time (i.e., the priest applying must be at least 60 years old). If one of these two criteria is met, the dispensation is granted quickly. If neither one is present, a dispensation is not granted. The pattern seems clear and real. For all practical purposes then, one must be of an advanced age or incapacitated at the time of ordination. The Pope seems to be intransigent on the matter."[18]

Continuing Catholics

What happens with a papal dispensation is that the wife may be married validly in the Church, even with a solemn nuptial Mass, but the Church does not recognize her as the wife of a priest. She is married to a layman, who has been officially pronounced a "non-priest" by the Church. The women we are studying in this survey were listed (with their husbands) in Martin Hegarty's Employment Bulletin, WEORC. Two out of five had been religious Sisters, most of them still in the convent when they met their future mates. The husbands were diocesan priests, ordained between 1968 and 1982, who had been active in the priesthood for an average of 6.4 years before resigning. They married rather promptly, most of them (84%) taking marriage vows within twelve months of the husband's resignation from the priesthood. Up to the time of this survey, in 1990, they had been married an average of 13.6 years.[19]

Many of the wives appear to be living in a kind of "twilight zone," where they are not sure of their identity as authentic Roman Catholics. Almost half (48%) had been married either in a civil ceremony or by a non-Catholic minister and there are still some (39%) whose marriages have not been "validated" by the Holy See. Some have been waiting more than ten years for word from Rome. About one-fifth of the husbands have not even bothered to apply for a dispensation from the Vatican. "Laicization," they now say, "is nothing more than an administrative detail." They know that the present Pontiff is extremely reluctant to grant the dispensation from celibacy. Nevertheless, almost all of the wives regularly attend Mass and the great majority "often" receive Holy Communion.

Whatever their "official" canonical status within the Church, they refuse to allow themselves to be completely "cut off" from the body of the faithful. Only one out of eight confesses to feeling "estranged" from the Church and a much smaller proportion are still alienated from their family for having "taken" a priest from his sacred ministry. They are ambivalent too about their identity as the "priest's wife." They tend to say, "I married a man, not a priest." Only about one-third of them consciously think of themselves as being the "wife of a priest." A smaller minority feel that marriage to a priest constitutes a kind of religious "calling" and a still smaller minority say that they themselves have a call to priestly ordination. In other words, they would like to present themselves generally in the simple role of normal married Catholic lay women.

Such generalizations obviously allow exceptions, like the wife who said, "Everything in me wants to shout that we are not different from other faithful wives. But, when I gather with married priests and their wives, I have to admit these are very special women. They do not think of themselves as being different because they are faithful, loving, supporting counterparts of the men they love, which is what every married woman should be, ideally. These women and the men they marry, however, have a holy urgency about them, because they are chosen by God. We share very deeply the struggle our spouses are experiencing in being denied and rejected."

Differential Dispensation

Most of the wives share the feeling that they and their husbands are under a kind of "punitive" cloud, even when there has been an "honorable discharge" from the priesthood. Their degree of frustration may be measured roughly by the manner in which the Holy See responded to the petition for release. Under Pope Paul VI the dispensation process went more smoothly than it did after his death in 1978. When we compared the men who left the active priesthood before 1975 with those who resigned later, we found that they were more than twice as likely (79% to 36%) to have received the dispensation from the Vatican.

The presence or absence of the rescript of dispensation has to affect the Catholic "status" of the wives of resigned priests who seek to live the normal life of a practicing Catholic. This in turn depends upon the vagaries of the Vatican. One wife said, "We were first married in 1969, but the dispensation arrived almost twenty years later, when we were married in the Church." The delays were much more numerous in later years. About two-thirds of the more recent resignees find themselves in an "invalid marriage," and thus technically "out of the Church."

Even with the limited survey data at hand, we are able to identify one category of women whose husbands left the priesthood but did not marry until they had received the dispensation. All of these valid marriages took place before 1978 and were witnessed by an active priest at a nuptial Mass. How do these marriages compare with those of men who did not wait for the rescript, or did not bother applying for it, and simply entered a civil contract or non-Catholic ceremony? The men who did not attempt marriage without a papal rescript had been in the priesthood for an average of 6.1 years before resigning. Their intention was to get married, but after leaving the priesthood they waited for 3.8 years until they received the dispensation from celibacy.

The men who are now in invalid marriages waited longer before resigning the ministry. They had been in the priesthood an average of 8.2 years and we have no explanation for this comparative delay of approximately two years. Having resigned, however, they were quicker to get married, waiting an average of 1.2 years. Since most of these marriages took place after John Paul became Pope, they may have been hurried by his refusal to grant permission. As a matter of fact, more than half (56%) did not even bother to apply for the dispensation.

Most of these clergy couples tend to continue their affiliation with the Catholic Church and they express a desire to return to the priestly ministry. The hopes and expectations of validly married couples tend to be higher than those of the people in the "bad" marriages. Eight out of ten say they desire restoration to the priesthood, but fewer (60%) really expect to be invited back "in our lifetime." The comparative answers for the invalidly wed are six out of ten (58%) who would like to return, but fewer (22%) who realistically expect the Vatican to change the rules.

Another interesting difference between these two categories of clergy couples is that the men in the valid marriages were more likely (51% to 31%) to have married women who had been religious Sisters. One can only guess whether these former nuns were influential in delaying the wedding with the resigning cleric until the dispensation was received. As they carry on their lives as Catholic parishioners, the wives in the valid marriages tend to act like faithful Catholic laity, frequently attending Mass and receiving the Eucharist. About four out of ten wives teach the CCD classes, act as Eucharistic ministers, and about half of them are lectors in the liturgy. The Bishop's attention is not on the wife, but on her husband, who should "take part in the life of the People of God. He should also give edification, and thus show himself to be a most loving son of the Church."[20]

It appears then that the clergy couples who are validly married are not distinguishable from "good" practicing Catholic lay folks. They are interested parishioners who tend to have friendly relations with their bishop and are in personal contact with the local clergy. In their continuing practice of the Catholic faith, the status of valid-versus-invalid marriages does not seem to make a difference. Approximately the same proportion (27% to 31%) report that their husbands occasionally celebrate Mass. They are also fairly similar in religious customs, saying grace before meals, meditating on the scriptures, receiving Holy Communion, and attending Mass.

Unblessed Marriages

The priests' wives who tend to feel uncomfortable in their marriage are those Catholic women whose husbands have not received the Vatican dispensation from celibacy. Some of them have lost interest in Catholicism: "We never officially left the Church but we don't go any more, and we found another interdenominational Church we now go to. Our children love it, and they don't get bored. The minister couple take turns weekly in the pulpit." This lady has no hope that the Church will change, but she and her husband had a kind of religious conversion: "We started praying on our own. We meditated every morning and found new meanings in the Bible."

Another woman angrily returned the survey questionnaire, on which she wrote: "I do not consider myself the 'wife of a priest' any longer (thanks to your Roman Catholic Bishops). Therefore, I'm not inclined to take part in this senseless survey." Very few wives leave the Church so completely, but some have a feeling of being "unwanted." They have little contact with the clergy and even less with the Bishop. Few of them are active in CORPUS, or even know anything about the Association. Nevertheless, six out of ten of these invalidly wed women would like to have their husbands "restored" to the priesthood, and one out of five thinks that ultimately the Vatican will have to accept a married clergy.

The tendency of these wives—and their husbands—is to drop out of the existing loose network of resigned priests. Those who have no expectation that the Vatican will change the celibacy rules prefer to be "left alone." Marital anonymity is the preference of the lady who disliked "having to 'hide' knowledge of our background at times, not being able to be open about a priest-husband for fear of judgment about our right or ability to function within the Church."

One wife who is attempting to live as a normal parishioner complained that, "our Bishop recently reminded our pastor that my husband and I (and other couples like us) were not to receive Holy Communion." Another remarks that in her part of the country "there are many people hostile to the men who have left. Because we have small children, we are very careful about sharing my husband's background. Others in our community who have not been as careful have suffered harassment from both the community and Church officials."

Offsetting these negative reactions is the considerable number of couples in "unblessed" marriages who claim to have no conscience problem about their canonical status: "We did everything according to proper form. We were convinced that a priest, like every other man, has a fundamental right to marriage. We took spiritual counseling with a monsignor, through whom we filled out the official papers to be sent to the Vatican. All the formalities were observed. Repeated requests for the rescript went unanswered, and we finally followed our conscience and got married." They usually "shop around" for a parish where the pastor takes a charitable view of their situation. These are the couples who attend Mass often and receive Communion. They send their children to the parochial school, are active in the Parent's Club and other parish activities. In the gatherings of the Association for a Married Priesthood, they do not identify themselves in a different category from the clergy couples who have received the dispensation from Rome.

The Continuing Priesthood

It is not easy for them to forget that their spouses are priests—nor do they want to. Most of them do not refer to their husbands as "ex-priests," or as "former" priests, but prefer the term, "non-canonical" priest, as it has been defined by theologian Anthony Padovano. In other words, their husbands have not ceased to be clergymen, but they are canonically prohibited from exercising the sacramental functions of the priesthood. One gets the impression, however, that this prohibition is being less carefully heeded with the passage of the years. Three out of ten of the wives report that their husbands "occasionally" celebrate the Eucharist, usually within the family circle, or in a small gathering of relatives and friends.

One way in which their sense of Catholic "belongingness" maintains itself is in the local gatherings of similar "non-canonical" couples. Sometimes they invite an "active" priest to celebrate the Mass with them and to conduct a spiritual or scriptural dialogue. In other groups the "reserve" priests themselves take turns in conducting the religious ceremony. This is the pattern followed in one large urban instance by a group of five clergy couples and their children who sometimes invite their close friends and neighbors to participate in the Mass. This practice seems to have become fairly common. At a large conference of married priests and their wives in 1988, a "show of hands" responding to this question indicated that approximately one-third of the priests present had said Mass "privately." What is happening in these circles is the confident assumption that "we remain priests of God regardless of any certification from the Vatican."

The feeling of isolation, or estrangement—to the extent that it may have previously existed—seems to be gradually disappearing. Contact among these couples, and their groups, has been increasing over recent years. The married couples of this study are aware that CORPUS (Corps of Reserve Priests United for Service) has been energetically reorganized and now speaks for them under its new name, the National Association for a Married Priesthood. Local groups of these clergy couples have been formed in more than seventy dioceses. They send representatives to the National Conventions and are now involved with the International Congress of Married Priests. The wives are becoming more active in the Association, which has elected two women to its National Board of Directors.

The respondents to this survey are well represented in COR-PUS membership. Seven out of ten (72%) are dues-paying members and almost as many of them (68%) want the organization to be more "aggressive" in pursuing its goals. They think also that the Vatican should change its rules and accept them officially as valid clergy couples. Most of them (61%), however, doubt that this change will occur "in our lifetime." Nevertheless, they leave little doubt that they want to be involved intimately in the functioning of the Church. In a cautious way, the majority (70%) desire a restoration into Church ministry as a "clergy couple," but only under certain conditions.

The obvious main condition under which they are willing to return to the Church ministry is that the husband be reinstated to the fullness of the priesthood and that they be recognized as validly married, with the Vatican assuring the sanctity of their marriage and the equality of women. This asks the Church to affirm two long-standing contentious issues: optional celibacy for clergy and equal status for women. Some of the more outspoken women are asking for a "reorganized" Church, modernized in management and authority, doing away with paternalism, clericalism, male chauvinism. "The last thing they want," says one wife, "is life in a typical parish rectory." Another insists on a Church that is "collegial, inclusive and visionary" as a genuine Christian community.

Life in the Parish

Although the majority of the wives attend Mass "often," only a minority take part in the life of the parochial community. In some instances the local pastor does not allow such participation of either wife or husband. In other instances, especially in smaller parishes, some of the wives (24%) are permitted to act as extraordinary ministers of the Eucharist, as lectors in the liturgy (30%), or as teachers in Confraternity of Christian Doctrine (23%). One of their frustrating experiences is to be in attendance at the Sunday Mass, at a "priestless" parish, where a deacon or religious Sister conducts the liturgical service, gives a homily and distributes Holy Communion.

One wife in a West Coast city parish marvels at what she calls a "clerical extravaganza," a local surplus of priests: "We have fifteen priests in our parish, ten married and five single." The largest parochial clergy concentration seems to be in Washington, D. C., where many married priests have gravitated over the decades since Vatican II: "We have six priests assigned to this religious-order parish, but in the congregation we have fourteen married priests and one married monsignor." By any measure of personnel utilization such concentrations of unused clerical manpower seem a waste of trained talent.

In the normal Catholic parish the attitude of the pastor toward the clergy couple ranges from warm friendliness to cold hostility. The clergy couple, however, has not been completely forsaken by the active priests of the diocese, especially former seminary classmates who remain a kind of "old boy" network in the larger cities. More than half (56%) of the wives said that they and their husbands are on friendly terms with "many" local diocesan priests. Their contact occurs usually in a casual and informal relationship. Some attempts are being made, however, to formalize these contacts and to organize regularly scheduled conferences between the active and the resigned clergy. Even in the few dioceses where the Bishop approves such gatherings (Austin, Corpus Christi, Great Falls, Indianapolis, Lansing, Marquette), the older and more conservative clergy still seem reluctant to associate with these priests and their wives. They appear anxious to avoid the impression that they approve the status of married priests.

Up to now very few of the wives of resigned priests have had personal contact with the married convert priests who were ordained into the Catholic priesthood through the "pastoral provisions."[21] Some make comments about the "double standard" that allows complete acceptance of convert married clergy, while excluding their own husbands who have resigned to marry. This is admittedly a "delicate" matter, spoken of only guardedly in public. Some bishops brusquely reject this comparison with the statement, "They asked for it; they got what they deserved." The leaders of CORPUS know that nothing is to be gained by antagonizing the hierarchy. Resentment is kept on a low key because the restoration of active clergy status has to depend largely on the goodwill of the bishops.[22]

While a small proportion of the wives admit that they stay aloof from the local clergy, a larger minority (31%) say that the Bishop wants nothing to do with them. As a matter of fact, the collective reaction of bishops has been highly inconsistent, ranging from cold exclusion and virtual ostracism in some dioceses to cordial and cooperative relations in others. "It's good to know that not all of the bishops are antagonistic. Our Bishop invites us to an annual dinner and social evening. He is sympathetic and cooperative, and hires as many married priests as he can place in the diocese." In another diocese, the bishop himself issued invitations to a discussion meeting between active and resigned priests, but found few "takers" among the active priests. As the "pinch" of the clergy shortage gets more insistent, the attitudes of some bishops begin to become more benevolent.

The Realistic Appraisal

When we asked them what they like most, and what they like least, about being married to a priest, we received a mixed set of responses. Although most of them wanted to concentrate on this *husband,* rather than on this *priest,* one enthusiastic wife said that "priests make the best husbands." Another went even further and boasted that, "if someone asked me to identify God, I would point to my husband." Marital devotion is expressed more often in terms of spiritual appreciation than of romantic attachment. The husband's religious character is admired by his wife: "The best thing in being married to my husband is that he is a kind, caring, loving person, but his priesthood is *not* responsible for that."

On the negative side, however, there is the rare wife who has a nagging "conscience problem" in recalling the hurt she caused her parents by this marriage. None of them expresses contrition or says that marrying a priest was the "wrong thing" to do. Yet, there is the occasional feeling of guilt that the rules have been broken, that it is better if people don't know who you are: "Having to hide the knowledge of our background at times. Not being able to be open about a priest-husband, for fear of judgments about our right, or ability, to function within the Church." The woman whose husband became an Episcopal priest resents the fact that "he works on my one day off." It should be noted that negative reactions are expressed by only a small number of the wives.

Many of the wives, however, are forthright enough to find fault with the seminary training and clerical experiences that made marriage and family a difficulty for their spouse. They thought that living in an exclusively male world for so long had blunted their husband's sensitivity to the needs of wife and children. As the Bishops' Survey suggested, "the seminary training, the years in the priesthood, and the emotional turmoil of resignation all combine to make the resignee less equipped to deal with the strains of the marital relationship."[23] One wife's only negative remark was that her husband "sleeps during sermons and then frequently comments that the sermon could be improved." Although the wives recognized such shortcomings, none of them expressed regret that she had married this husband.

Every couple is willing to admit that "adjustments" were needed in the first years of their marriage. From the age perspective of the priests theirs was a "mature" marriage from the beginning, and most of the women were over thirty when they entered marriage. It should be noted that many of the wives who had been nuns for ten to fifteen years had also developed personal characteristics that were non-marital. In other words, they had lived in the midst of a "female culture" that was in no way preparatory for marriage. Having gone through the novitiate and convent training for a life of virginity, they were least prepared for married life.

One wife ruefully admitted that "after seventeen years in religious life it was like a shock to get married. Having three children in my thirties was the last thing I could have anticipated while in the convent." It is sometimes said that a man "never forgets" he is a priest. More than one married priest says that his wife has "never forgotten that she was a nun." The behavior patterns of long years in the celibate convent do not easily wear off. The regularity of life, the attention to details, the "fussiness" of the convent schedule, are not the best preparation for the marital routine and family living. It is true, of course, that among our respondents more than half of these wives had not been convent-trained, or members of religious Sisterhoods.

Continuing Ministry

One of the "smoothest" cooperative marriages I have discovered is that of wife and husband who had both been in the parish educational ministry before their marriage. In their marriage experience they had no need to "adjust" to each other because of spiritual background. They felt that they had parallel backgrounds, she in the convent, he in the seminary. Her subsequent experience in a parish seemed quite similar to his ministry as assistant pastor. By great good fortune, after they married, they were hired as a "team" for the direction of religious education. In other words, neither of them was called upon to do liturgical or sacramental tasks. It must be pointed out that the majority of resigned priests are not employed by any church-related institution, even though their wives may be more occupied in chores around the parish. On the other hand, the desire for pastoral ministry was so strong in a minority of the couples that they switched church affiliation, mainly to Lutheran, Methodist and Episcopalian.

In more than one situation married priests have undertaken to serve as co-pastors in Protestant Churches. A Congregational

Church in New Jersey is now "served by a pastoral team of three married priests and a Protestant pastor. An additional four ordained Protestants and one married Catholic priest are members of the church."[24] The wives also participate fully in these Protestant parishes which tend to be called "inclusive" rather than "ecumenical," because they are open to the un-churched as well as to members of other denominations.

The earlier strictures that had been placed on resigned priests and their wives have gradually been lifted. One of the reasons is that there are now so many who simply "refuse to disappear." Even the priest who obtains a dispensation is no longer willing to accept the bishops' decree that he must "keep silent" about his priesthood and must move his residence away from his friends and family. There is the further fact that many of these men, and their wives, refuse to make a complete break with the dedicated ministry. Many are ready to say that "we are together in the service of the Lord."

It is no longer "unheard of" that a married priest is hired to teach in a Catholic college or high school, to work in diocesan institutions, even the chancery office. They are in Catholic char-ities, in drug and alcoholic rehabilitation, in mental health, and family counseling. Similarly, many of the wives are engaged in Catholic hospitals, social work, child care, education, and other of the helping ministries. Within the Catholic Church itself, al-most half of the men (47%) and more than one-third (37%) of the women are engaged in varieties of the helping apostolates.

What seems potentially significant for a growing ministry on the part of married priests and their wives is the tacit approval detected on the part of many bishops. More than a third of the respondents to this survey say that the bishops they know are quietly and privately providing job opportunities for resigned priests and their wives. They apply for jobs that have normally been held by the clergy or by religious Sisters. What had once been barely "allowed" has now become routine in the face of personnel shortage. Clerical couples are in many dioceses tak-ing the place of the very people whose resignations had created the shortage of priests and religious.

Endnotes

1. She and many other clergy wives were celebrated by Roland Bainton, *Women of the Reformation,* Minneapolis, Augsburg, 1977.

2. In the light of improved ecumenical relations the name of this periodical was changed to *Christian Heritage,* in April, 1958.

3. See Charles Davis, *A Question of Conscience,* New York, Harper & Row, 1967. See also, Joseph Fichter, *A Sociologist Looks at Religion,* Wilmington, Glazier, 1988, chapter 13, "Vanishing Church Professionals."

4. George H. Frein, "For the Love of Jeanne," pp. 85-98, in John A. O'Brien, ed., *Why Priests Leave,* New York, Hawthorne, 1969.

5. Both are listed with Dissertation Abstracts International and are available through University Microfilms.

6. This *Directory* has 1,060 entries, far short of the dues-paying membership of CORPUS.

7. The WEORC *Directory* lists many resigned priests who are not members of CORPUS, and not necessarily seeking to return to the active ministry.

8. Maureen Hendricks, *A Study of the Marriages and Marital Adjustment of Resigned Roman Catholic Priests and Their Wives* (unpublished Dissertation), Greeley, University of Northern Colorado, 1979. Chapter 2, "Methodology," and chapter 7, "Discussion of Findings."

9. James Gill, "Despondence: Why We See It in Priests," *Medical Insight,* December, 1969, pp. 31-32.

10. *The Catholic Priest in the United States: Sociological Investigations,* Washington, United States Catholic Conference, pp. 293-298.

11. Hendricks, *op. cit.,* p. 22.

12. *Ibid.,* pp. 76-77.

13. *Ibid.,* pp. 91-92, 109.

14. The Council of Trent declared "anathema" to anyone who says that you can be happier as a married person, than as a celibate or virgin.

15. Joseph H. Fichter, *The Pastoral Provisions*, Kansas City, Sheed & Ward, 1989, p. 30.

16. *Ibid.,* p. 57.

17. "Involvement of Dispensed Priests in the Official Ministry of the Church," *The Jurist,* 34, 2, (1974), pp. 143-153.

18. Report on "Laicization Process" to NCCB Sub-Committee on Priestly Affirmation and Support, September 26, 1983.

19. Joseph H. Fichter, "Wives Speak About Life with Father," *National Catholic Reporter*, March 23, 1990, pp. 24-25.

20. "Involvement of Dispensed Priests," *The Jurist, op. cit.,* p. 152.

21. Joseph H. Fichter, *The Pastoral Provisions*, Kansas City, Sheed & Ward, 1989, pp. 56-57.

22. In a pastoral letter of January 7, 1991, Archbishop Rembert Weakland declared himself willing to ask the Pope to ordain a married man. See Pat Windsor's Report, *National Catholic Reporter,* January 18, 1991, p. 3. Four Cardinals have also called for a married priesthood: Arns of Brazil, Darmojuwono of Indonesia, Hume of England, and Pellegrino of Italy.

23. Bishops' Study, *op. cit.,* p. 296.

24. Anne L. Hess, "Catholics and Protestants in a UCC Church," *The Christian Century*, April 18, 1990, pp. 401-402.

Chapter Eight

Long Engagements

Every child growing up in a typical Roman Catholic family knew that there were some people who did not get married. Some stayed single because they did not want to marry, others because nobody wanted to marry them. A bachelor uncle would show up for Thanksgiving Day dinner. A maiden aunt might help the children with their homework. She was sometimes called an "old maid," or even a "spinster." She might fall in love with the new young assistant at church, but he was not allowed to fall in love with her. He was different and so were the Sisters who taught in the parochial school. Every Catholic knew that Sisters and priests simply did not get married.

This traditional and orderly distinction between lay people and celibate priests, religious Sisters and Brothers, came into question soon after the Second Vatican Council. In dealing with the evangelical counsels of chastity, the Council fathers said that "Church authority has the duty to interpret and regulate their practices." (*Lumen Gentium,* art. 43) This was understood by many as an invitation to relax the rigid separation between female and male religious, to foster casual heterosexual friendships, and to end the "artificial isolation" of seminarians from women. It was interpreted by some as permission to develop intimate, but non-conjugal, heterosexual friendships. There could even be a "Third Way" to actualize such relationships.

In the religious euphoria following the Second Vatican Council, one might well ask whether celibates could find in the institutional Church either a source or an instrument of the deep human sharing of personal love. One priest-psychologist suggested that "the present structures of priestly and religious life leave little room for the conscious expression of healthy and holy love in the Spirit between consecrated men and women." In simplest terms, the Church did not allow its most dedicated servants to fall in love, for fear they would want to marry. "Throughout the world there are thousands of priests and religious who are confronting the contradiction of seemingly loveless structures that go by grand but empty names."[1]

In December, 1967, Pedro Arrupe, General of the Society of Jesus, made it clear that there was no room for any Jesuit practitioner of the *via tertia*, which cannot be justified or approved by either the Council or the Jesuit Constitutions. "We cannot permit the cultivation of an exclusive and intimate friendship with a woman, in which the couple manifest to each other their secret soul with their most personal emotions and desires, and dedicate their persons in an analogous marriage, but which excludes the conjugal privileges."[2] He concluded that any Jesuit practitioner of the "Third Way" must be dismissed from the Society.

It appears that some of the younger women religious were getting interested in prospective companionship with seminarians and priests. Articles and editorials began to appear with some regularity in *Sisters Today*, the popular periodical written for nuns and read mainly by them. These writings were a warning about moral temptations of such friendships, but without an ultimate condemnation of male-female relationships. Since the Third Way focused on liaisons between dedicated celibates, it was obviously a matter of concern to the leaders and authorities of religious women's congregations.

Sandra Schneiders sees the issue of sexual abstinence as an urgent problem for many religious women. Is it "permissible under some circumstances," she asks, "for a religious with a public vow of consecrated celibacy to maintain a responsible, private, genitally expressed relationship with someone, provided it causes no scandal and does not harm either party, or their other relationships, and does not interfere with their primary community and ministerial commitments? This arrangement is sometimes referred to as the Third Way."[3] Her answer, of course, is in the negative. This kind of relationship is not a "viable option."

News of the first collective "breakthrough" came from Holland, where some Dutch priests got married and insisted that they continue their regular ministry in the parish. They could not easily be dismissed by the Bishops, because Dutch law stipulates that "you cannot fire a man because he married." Other priests who fell in love, but did not want to commit themselves to marriage, invented what they called the "Third Way." The Dutch Bishops eventually took notice of this phenomenon at their special Synod in Rome and declared that, "with regard to a sort of Third Way, lived as an ambiguous state between celibacy and marriage, the members of the Synod are unanimous in rejecting it."[4]

Third Way

The practical implementation of the so-called "Third Way," as rejected by the Jesuit General and by the Bishops of Holland, apparently evolved from a type of relationship described thirty years earlier by Pierre Teilhard de Chardin. He speculated that "between marriage, always socially polarized on the basis of reproduction, and religious perfection, theologically presented in terms of separation, we decidedly need a Third Way (I do not say a middle, but superior)—way demanded by the revolutionary transformation which has recently occurred in our thought by the transposition of the notion of 'spirit.'" He had already speculated about the "Eternal Feminine" and about the "Evolution of Chastity," in which he celebrated "the advantages of non-physical but 'passionate' friendship between the sexes."[5]

Teilhard enjoyed the friendship of many women who found him personally attractive. He readily accepted assistance from them. The "special" woman for whom he had the deepest devotion was Lucille Swan, an American divorced sculptress, who fell deeply in love with him. When she met him in China she considered him "one of the most fascinating men I ever met." His insistence that their love must be sublimated was nonsense to her. She was almost forty when they first met, but after a few weeks of seeing him daily she began to "feel young and full of hope again." They discussed the question of celibacy and marriage, but his explanations seemed silly to her. Her expectation of marriage with him was finally thwarted.

Another well-known instance of the Third Way was the romantic love shared by Thomas Merton and nurse "S," with whom he talked about the possibility of getting married. He told his friend, Wilbur Ferry, "what I want to do is go away with this woman for a month. Just for a month. What do you think of that?"[6] In his journal, in March, 1967, he recalled the anniversary of the "rainy evening when [S] came to say good-bye before going to Chicago, and when I was so terribly lonely, lay awake half the night, tormented by the gradual realization that we were in love and I did not know how I could live without her."[7] Love letters were exchanged, love poems written, surreptitious visits made with her, and secret phone calls. His friends tried to dissuade him, but one of his phone calls was overheard and reported to the Abbot. Word got around the monastery and he wondered how many monks looked upon him as a "priest who has a woman."

The Third Way is a love relationship, but by definition it allows no room for physical intimacy beyond what occurs between sister and brother in a healthy Christian family. In the old days, when excommunication was the penalty for the married priest and his wife, reconciliation and a return to the sacraments could be granted only under the condition that the couple "live as brother and sister." In Teilhard's description, the intense celibate-love relationship cannot be an exclusive relationship, even in the sense of a "spiritual marriage," because it is "superior" to any kind of human conjuncture. It presumes a mature and firm sense of vocation and selfless fulfillment. The focus of this love transcends the beloved and "seeks to share with as many as possible the same love out of which it is born."[8]

Celibate *Caritas*

Eugene Kennedy uses the term, "celibate love," and warns about the "difficulties and dangers of making room for human love of this order in the lives of priests, religious, and the apostolic laity." The Third Way is a transcendent gift of the Spirit that is not intended simply for the personal fulfillment of the individual who experiences it. Secondly, it is not given solely for the mutual enjoyment of the couple who have received it, but for the sake of the Church. Thirdly, the whole meaning of this gift of love is to develop fully the personhood of the Church's servants, so that "their gift of themselves to the People of God will be as total and effective as possible."[9] The mutual love that attracted two celibates to each other becomes a communal and all-embracing love.

Here, Schillebeeckx returns to the Synod of Dutch Bishops in Rome and asks precisely what the Bishops meant when they banned the Third Way. He points out that historically the law of celibacy was essentially a law of abstinence, but was not concerned with the presence, or absence, of love between a man and a woman. The real heart of the problem of celibacy in the modern context has to go deeper than the notion that it is nothing more than a kind of "shared abstinence." If we interpret this Synod "along the lines of 'shared celibacy' (with a view to complete abstinence), then for the first time in the history of the Church, or at least in the Church's legislation, we have a pronouncement which is completely new; viz., that it is the nature of celibacy to exclude not only sexuality but also the 'love of a woman.'" He is reluctant to allow a Synod in a particular country "to make a decision on the nature of the charism of celibacy, which differed radically from anything that had happened before in Church history!"[10]

The transcendent love that characterizes the Third Way is expressive of the central virtue of the Christian religion, a genuine *caritas* that reaches out even to one's enemy. (Mt. 5:43) The person who is dedicated to God's service is expected to exercise this universal love. The parish is a large family and the priest loves everybody in the family. Yet, it is a common experience of parish life that the pastor visits some families more than others and develops particular friendships among them. Parishioners generally consider this a wholesome way of assuaging the loneliness that everyone recognizes in the priest's life. There are almost always some families who are "close" to the clergy in the manner of a pleasant Christian fellowship.

In 1982 the Bishops' Committee on Priestly Life and Ministry said that "central to priesthood is the call to friendship." Relatedness to others is at the heart of human life, even though aloneness is part of the demand of the celibate life. Women are most active in the parish groups and their presence must be recognized. "Many priests, like many other men, have experienced the complementing role of a good woman friend in their lives. We're beginning to see competent women brought onto staffs in seminaries and houses of formation for men religious, precisely so that young men in training for priestly ministry may have the benefit of broader ministerial role models."[11]

Several realistic scenarios were presented in the "Reflection Guide," concerning the development of the personal friendship of a parish priest and a religious Sister. Subsequent stages of this relationship are described. "Father Mark found that getting close to someone made him vulnerable to criticism, in a way new to his experience. He felt he was more in touch with a whole range of feelings, his own and others." A few months later, Mark was having second thoughts: "There was a dynamic at work that wasn't subject to neat planning. She was a part of his life he felt more and more wary about sharing with anyone. Sister Mary found this attitude hard; she seemed insulted by it." The critical stage was the point at which he was assigned as pastor to a distant parish. Sister Mary "fell apart! Try as he might to point out the inevitability of this move, she couldn't seem to reconcile herself to seeing him only infrequently." Mark confided this reaction to his own sister who told him, "You have to understand that relationships are different for a woman."[12]

Friendship

At what level of intensity may this particular kind of friendship exist and develop between the priest and his women parishioners? At what point does she feel in need of special attention? There is no question that women are the most active and most dedicated parishioners and tend to meet the pastor with some frequency. One resigned priest remarks admiringly that "some priests whom I know personally are deeply in love with beautifully dedicated Christian women whom they have met, usually by chance, in the course of their ministry. I admire endlessly their ability to maintain frequent, if not daily, contact with these women through phone calls and letters, without letting it distract from their celibate commitment to the whole people of God."[13]

Lucy Beckett asserts that "holy and creative friendship between celibate men and women is a much-to-be-treasured Catholic pattern, which depends for its value on a shared recognition of male/female equality before God. Jerome and Paula, Francis of Sales and Jane de Chantal, Teresa of Avila and John of the Cross: Only a thoroughly secular, post-Freudian understanding of sexuality can detract from the Christian, and actually specifically Catholic, significance of these relationships."[14]

People in such close friendships may consciously avoid the moral dilemma of "falling in love" in the secular erotic definition. In their moments of calm rationality they know that this is a "no win" situation. If he is to remain a priest "in good standing," he simply cannot commit himself to a love relationship of sexual intimacy. The woman who is a faithful and "practicing" Catholic, and intends to remain one, knows that she cannot simultaneously have an affair with a priest. If the personal friendship is to endure, it has to be maintained on the level of "Platonic" love, which is defined as "a close relationship between two persons, in which sexual desire has been suppressed or sublimated."

Platonic friendship, like the Third Way, does not always exist, and for everybody, at the same low level of emotional intensity. The concept of non-sexual friendship is meant to bridge the gap between celibacy and marriage.[15] People in training for a life of dedicated celibacy have always been warned of the "dangers" of associating with the opposite sex. Convent rules and monastic regulations always forbade the celibate to be alone, together with a member of the opposite sex. There are, however, no statistics to demonstrate the extent to which the Third Way succeeded, or failed, among seminarians and young religious Sisters of the '70's.

The point at which platonic love evolves into romantic love can best—and perhaps only—be described by the person who experiences it. For some, however, the experience is "love at first sight," like the priest's wife who said, "there was electricity between us from the beginning." For the most part, however, the love commitment tends to be a slow, hesitant, even tortuous discovery that "this is happening to us." The decision to leave the priesthood and marry is usually a soul-searching, painful experience, shared by the prospective bride. "I broke it off and left the country for a summer of volunteer work in Peru. When I came back, his letters were there, telling me that 'our love will never die.'" Apparently distance is an effective solution only if the couple remain distant.

Proximity seems to be a relentless factor in the evolution from platonic love to romantic love. The resolution to stay apart and to "call it off" is, of course, the "rational" answer to the unsolved dilemma of continence versus marriage. As one wife remarked, "Unless they can both refrain from the painful desire to be physically united in the full expression of their love, it is almost impossible to continue in an intimate relationship." An experienced priest who tried to maintain a "sexless" companionship finally declared his conviction that, "a priest committed to celibacy and a woman with the vow of virginity cannot support a deep emotional involvement without opting for marriage or agreeing to drift apart."[16]

Courtship

Many of the priests' wives who had been nuns met their future husband while they were still in the religious Sisterhood. Some of them "dated" while in the convent, and even became engaged while he was still in the priesthood. Not every man who resigns from the priesthood does so in order to marry, but those who do marry follow roughly the pattern sequence that is common to the American culture: You meet an attractive woman, get to know each other in shared activities, fall in love, and become engaged to marry. One exceptional instance is that of the priest who reversed this procedure: "As a priest who wanted to stay a priest, I had to find someone who would also love me as a priest and who would share my interest in the ministry." He says he looked for, and found, a girl willing to marry him, but "we began to date only after we became engaged."[17]

It is the exceptional married priest who did not meet his future wife until after he had resigned the active ministry. In the great majority of cases the "courtship" began while he was still functioning in the clergy. In her excellent 1979 study of marital adjustment in Catholic clergy marriages, Maureen Hendricks found that three-quarters of the wives had gone on dates while their future husbands were still engaged in the ministry and more than one-third became engaged before he resigned.[18] Regardless of when they began to date, the average length of time they spent "going steady" was about a year and a half before getting married.

We have no way of knowing how many promises were broken or how many engagements made by priests did not eventuate in a wedding. The couple is in love, the mutual commitments have been declared, but as time passes it is usually the priest who wavers. Often there is great emotional turmoil as he hesitates to take that final step: "You know I want to leave and marry you, but I'm afraid." Or, he may say, "I can't do this while my mother is still alive. It would break her heart." He may be holding back while waiting for the dispensation from the Vatican, even though he knows that such documents are now rarely granted. Meanwhile, the engagement tends to drift into an "affair."

The need to "sneak around" and avoid discovery is distasteful and embarrassing for the couple who are not supposed to be in love. One wife wrote quite frankly: "I'm thirty-nine years old and have been married to a priest for fourteen years. We have four children. At the time when we realized how deep and intimate our relationship had become, we were fearful that we'd be discovered, that we'd lose our reputation and be disgraced, and be misunderstood by family, friends and relatives. We could get together only in secret and always in the fear of being found out. So it was a great relief and a blessing when we decided to emerge from anonymity and get married."

The fact that such love liaisons are forbidden by the Church and disapproved by the faithful makes more difficult the final decision to resign the priesthood and marry. After all, the woman fell in love with a priest whom she admires for what he is and for what he represents. The effort to disentangle the man from his role causes ambivalence in the mind of the woman he loves. She realizes that all this will change. "He will no longer be the man I now so deeply admire and appreciate, if he gives up his priesthood." The couple by this time has exchanged some kind of vows and the longer they delay, the more difficult their effort to avoid sexual intimacy. The longer the engagement, the stronger the erotic impulse. If sexual intimacy ensues, it usually begins about a year into the relationship and becomes a kind of "common-law" marriage.

Romantic Affairs

An article in the *National Catholic Reporter* in 1986 began with the words: "One of the least-kept secrets around is that a number of U. S. priests have love affairs with women." Secrecy and anonymity are almost essential for these relationships, with the result that the number of such cases cannot be known. Yet, it may be said that, "whether these women tell stories of anger or guilt, whether they speak out of acute loneliness, to help other women or to aid in ending mandatory celibacy, the result is that for the first time the dynamics of these affairs are becoming visible."[19]

Women who are intimate with priests demand a promise of anonymity before talking about their relationship. One exception was the appearance of Maggie Olsen on the Phil Donahue Show in 1985. She spoke of her own relationship as a "non-consummated friendship" with a priest whom she dearly loved, but who broke off the relationship to her sorrow. This publicity brought her to the attention of other women—and some priests—who were at varying degrees of cohabitation and "needed somebody to talk to." With the help of sympathetic clergy couples she set up an informal group called "Good Tidings," that soon included a loose network of psychological consultants ready to volunteer assistance. About 700 women, and almost one-third as many priests, have called in to discuss their uncomfortable love relationships.

"Good Tidings" continues under the quiet and devoted sponsorship of Joseph and Catherine Grenier, who point out that "since the conflict is not usually one of faith, we encourage them to resolve their problem within the Catholic Church. Sometimes we feel it necessary to encourage a victimized woman to seek legal redress (for child support, for example) when simple justice is not possible within the Church." While publicity is shunted from the cohabiting couple, Good Tidings feels it important to make the institutional Church more aware of this issue "and of the large numbers of priests caught up in relationships which often cause serious harm to them and to women, and which ultimately involve issues of justice—and often legal problems as well—for the Church. We do our best to cooperate with the institutional church in finding humane and just solutions to this problem."

According to Beifuss, what is most surprising is the "length of many of these attachments. The women speak of the relationships continuing for two years, five years, eight years." As long as the priest remains in the active ministry, these long-term relationships are maintained in the greatest secrecy, although there are often fellow clergy who know (or suspect) but who "look the other way." Both the priest and his paramour have to arrange their life-styles to make the relationship workable. Most often their assignation is on the priest's day off and at a distant motel. One frequent remark is that "we always take our vacation together." The frequency of such contacts varies widely. One woman complained that, "I hardly ever see him," but another reported she "was able to be with her lover two or three times a week for four- or five-hour stretches—although she pointed out that he was not a parish priest."

The women who call for help from Good Tidings are "going steady" with a priest, are not promiscuous, nor are they involved in an occasional "one-night stand." Whatever the relationship is called, it is clearly a violation of clerical celibacy. Since it is deliberately shrouded in secrecy, we cannot speak with certainty about the numbers of priests involved. The largest estimate I know of comes from a resigned priest, A.W. Richard Sipe, a psychotherapist who has drawn information from approximately 1,500 persons over the past quarter-century. He estimates that about twenty percent of priests are involved in a "rather well-defined non-celibate relationship with a woman." He estimates further, that a small proportion (6% to 8%) "experiment with non-celibacy." They intend to remain celibate but "waver and engage in dating-like behavior."[20]

It appears that the Catholic Church in Germany is experiencing a more open, and more frequent, pattern of clergy love affairs than is the case in the United States. Eugen Drewermann, a priest-theologian in Paderborn, published a psychological study of the German Catholic clergy, in which he asserts that one-third of the priests in Germany are living in concubinage.[21] He claims that this practice is so widespread that it no longer causes scandal among the faithful. The author himself is not negatively critical of this phenomenon. On the contrary, he suggests that the love relation with a woman results in a better, and more mature, priesthood. He has been subjected to severe criticism by his ecclesiastical superior, Archbishop Johannes Degenhardt.

Another, and much longer, account is provided by more than thirty German women who are emotionally involved with Catholic priests. Seven of them were jilted by their priest lovers; others established a stable family life with children. "Carola" gives excerpts from the journal she kept, from December, 1980, to February, 1983, when she finally married her man. Some simply cohabited without benefit of wedding vows, like "Sabine," who wrote that "we who keep our love affair secret and do not marry our partner are really stabilizing the system of celibacy. I sometimes think that if all the priests who are living with a woman were to make this public, the hierarchy could no longer insist on clerical celibacy."[22] The women who contributed essays to this book are associated with the German version of "Good Tidings," but with the title, *Initiativegruppe der vom Zolibat betroffenen Frauen.*

Espousals

The autobiographical book by Michael Miles, *Love is Always,* is described on the dust jacket as "the unprecedented account of the only man in American history openly to marry and begin a family without forfeiting his position as a priest." Although his congregation wanted to keep him as their married pastor, his Bishop finally put an end to the arrangement and dismissed him. Father Miles appealed to Pope John Paul II in the following words: "You alone are the shepherd who may initiate a process in the future toward the reconciliation of thousands of your priest brothers now suffering in exile." The response came a year later in a brief message from the Papal Secretariat, promising that "His Holiness will remember you in his prayers."[23]

The expectation that a priest and his wife could function officially in a pastoral parochial ministry seems to be forlorn hope. Even the married priests who transferred from the Episcopal Church are not assigned to the regular *cura animarum* in the parish ministry. In the current circumstances of Vatican prohibitions, a resigned priest and his wife could hardly expect the Bishop's appointment, although one occasionally hears rumors that a bishop may ignore such a marital pastoral arrangement, if everybody "keeps quiet about it." Secret marriages of priests are said to occur among military chaplains who can remain undetected for many years and during shifts of assignments. "He's been married for seventeen years, has four children, and remains a Catholic military chaplain in good standing."

As the priest and his wife grow older, they settle into a kind of "Darby and Joan" relationship of trust and fidelity. One of my informants said, "We're talking about twenty-five years of committed marriage, with the mortgage paid off and children in college." They have grown to accept what was once considered a risky dual existence. "But you also have active relationships on the part of men and women who are emotionally committed to one another but are not living together. The men just won't give up their priesthood. They feel trapped." Yet, in some instances this kind of exclusive relationship is maintained over many years.

There are some cases—apparently rare—of enduring relationships, in which neither partner feels at fault, nor do they admit to a "conscience problem." For twenty years this priest had an ongoing relationship with a professional woman in town. They always met at her home, and they were always discrete—without being furtive—about their meetings. The relationship had been sexualized to the satisfaction of both. She was very active and successful in her profession. She was the kind of woman who did not want to be a mother and have the responsibilities of a household and children. She never asked him to leave the priesthood and marry her. This really suited both of them "right down to the ground." In the opinion of their mutually shared analyst, "it was a source of extreme mutual nourishment at all levels—intellectual, spiritual, emotional, and physical."

Despite these examples of long-term fidelity, there are also some instances of separation and divorce, perhaps better defined as desertion or abandonment. The sophisticated way to do this is to have an "amicable" separation, but some couples break up in public scandal. If the woman brings a paternity suit against her priest lover, she "may be paid off and told to go away." The diocesan attitude may be that "she played, so she pays." The priest goes back to the diocese, does his penance, gets a change of assignment, and gives her five thousand dollars on the promise not to prosecute him. As one deserted wife remarked, "the Church could continue to care for him, but he could not care for me, so he gave me the boot. Harder than loving in secret has been mourning in secret."[24]

In the face of growing evidence of these forbidden romances, one appreciates forthright feminist anger at the patriarchal male-dominated Roman Church. Over and over again, it is the woman who "pays and pays and pays." Women who willingly enter these "unholy" espousals are labelled as sinful persons, and when the affair breaks up they are the "losers." As one wife writes, "we are the victims of a church law that is non-biblical and historically outdated. We feel abused and have little self-esteem left, after being refused the dignity and title of wife." Another wife who was abandoned complains that "the law of celibacy has made it impossible to love fully, and has forced this kind of behavior to which men and women have resorted."

An outraged victim of clergy infidelity inveighs against the hypocrites who pretend that they are chaste. "I become very angry at those priests who feign celibacy, who live a lie and a very comfortable existence, and are so treasured by Rome because they have been faithful enough not to marry. They seem to have the best of both worlds and are very satisfied with that. Mandatory celibacy is not an issue with them. It is a safeguard for them and gives them carte blanche to 'any woman in the parish,' as one priest put it to a young man he was inviting to consider the priesthood. So, obligatory celibacy becomes a protective coating for the secret philanderer."

Women's Place

The common aggravation among Catholic feminists is that they have not been treated as free and equal members of the Church. In the so-called "illicit" relationship between a woman and a priest it is almost always the woman who is "at fault." In spite of the wave of liberation that has attracted even women religious, there is still a male tendency to demean the females. The most outspoken among the wives of CORPUS priests state very clearly that "there is little or no place within the structure of CORPUS for men and women who believe in a discipleship of equals, and who wish to spend their best energies working toward this goal. Unless CORPUS expands its horizons it will be difficult for women who realize their human and ecclesial dignity to be enthusiastically supportive."

For many years, the single goal of CORPUS was to gain recognition of a Catholic married priesthood and the restoration of its clergy membership to the active ministry. As late as July, 1988, Frank McGrath wrote in the CORPUS *Newsletter*: "A survey indicated that a slight majority of CORPUS priests favored the ordination of women. Others were opposed, but all agreed that it was not our cause." A circuitous approach to the role of women in the organization was developed in a session of the 1989 Columbus Conference "to explore the gifts women bring to a married priesthood." This, of course, puts the wife at the dedicated service of her clergy husband without establishing a place for herself.

It is taken for granted that the married priest is enlightened enough to treat his wife as an equal, but as a CORPUS member he faces a dilemma. The exclusive request for episcopal acceptance of the married priesthood can be complicated by the simultaneous promotion of women's ordination. Very few bishops are open to the suggestion of women priests and most of them share the typical chauvinist attitude toward women. The male tendency is to say that women's liberation, and not the *aggiornamento* of Vatican II, prepared the way for many priests to opt for marriage.

Several of the more vocal of the clergy wives suggest that we are asking the wrong question when talking about equal rights for women. Theoretically that battle has been won. After all, even the American Bishops have come out strongly for the rights of women in the Catholic Church. Sexism and clericalism are now condemned. A perceptive wife said that the love relationship goes beyond equality between the partners and recommends Gilligan's observation: "At a time when efforts are being made to eradicate discrimination between the sexes, in the search for social equality and justice, the differences between the sexes are being rediscovered in the social sciences."[25]

Quite aside from gender equality, the difference involved in the love relationship is that the experience is much deeper and more intense for the woman than for the man. In promoting equal opportunity and justice for women we tend to talk in terms of androgyny, that is, of human qualities enjoyed by both sexes. Men can be tender and women can be strong; thus, human qualities are shared across gender lines. Nevertheless, as one wife sagely remarked: "The emotional response inspired in the woman carries the expectation of exclusivity and permanence. If the man remains cool she feels exploited. Even if the man responds in love and loyalty, he is not likely to share the same level of intensity."

If the love experience is more intense for the woman than for the man, she is more ready for marriage than he is and less ready to "call it quits" when his ardor cools. One mature woman said, "I fell in love and I chased him for almost a year. It was great while it lasted, but he almost worried himself to death and decided to stay a priest." This woman spoke flippantly but was devastated at the breakup of her affair. Even if the man initiated the friendship, the woman responds with greater intensity and is much more affected by the breakup. She is likely to cling to the relationship, to foster its memories, to get hurt feelings, and to feel as though she has been unjustly treated.

Endnotes

1. Eugene C. Kennedy, "A Quiet Catholic Question," *America*, January 28, 1967, pp. 147-148.

2. *Acta Romana Societatis Jesu*, vol. xv, 1968, pp. 179-180.

3. Sandra Schneiders, *New Wineskins: Reimaging Religious Life Today,* New York, Paulist, 1986, p. 215.

4. "Dutch Synod Concludes," art. 32, *Origins,* vol. 9, no. 35, July 14, 1980, pp. 557-565.

5. Mary and Ellen Lukas, *Teilhard,* Garden City, Doubleday, 1977, p. 132, and passim.

6. W.H. Ferry, "Merton the Friend," pp. 87-93, in Paul Wilkes, ed., *Merton By Those Who Knew Him Best,* San Francisco, Harper & Row, 1984.

7. Michael Mott, *The Seven Mountains of Thomas Merton,* Boston, Houghton Mifflin, 1984, pp. 435-454, and passim.

8. Richard W. Kropf, "The Third Way," *Sisters Today,* vol. 47, January, 1976, pp. 264-271.

9. Eugene Kennedy, *Fashion Me A People: Man, Woman and the Church,* New York, Sheed & Ward, 1967, p. 105.

10. Edward Schillebeeckx, *The Church with a Human Face,* New York, Crossroad, 1985, p. 250.

11. *Human Sexuality and the Ordained Priesthood,* Committee on Priestly Life and Ministry, Washington, U. S. Catholic Conference, 1982, p. 47.

12. *Ibid.,* pp. 46-49.

13. George L. Weber, "I Heard A Voice," pp. 151-163, in John A. O'Brien, ed., *Why Priests Leave,* New York, Hawthorn, 1969.

14. Lucy Beckett, "The Essential Feminine," *The Evangelical Catholic,* October, 1990, p. 4 (Reprinted from *The Tablet*).

15. See Matthias Neuman, "Friendships between Men and Women in Religious Life," *Sisters Today,* vol. 46, October, 1974, pp. 81-93.

16. Weber, *op. cit.,* p. 160.

17. Carl J. Hemmer, "A Priest Who Didn't Leave," in John A. O'Brien, ed., *op. cit.,* pp. 140-150.

18. Maureen Hendricks, *A Study of the Marriage and Marital Adjustment of Resigned Roman Catholic Priests and Their Wives.* (Unpublished Dissertation) University of Northern Colorado, 1979, p. 76.

19. Joan Turner Beifuss, "Priests and Women in Love," *National Catholic Reporter*, July 18, 1986, pp. 18-19.

20. A. W. Richard Sipe, "A Secret World: Sexuality and the Search for Celibacy," reviewed by Pat Winsor, *National Catholic Reporter*, August 24, 1990, p. 6.

21. Eugen Drewermann, *Kleriker: Psychogramm eines Ideals*, Freiburg, Walter Verlag, 1989. His study was also discussed in the Rome-based periodical, *30 Days*, December, 1989, p. 29.

22. Sabine, "Schlusswort," pp. 372ff, in Anne Lueg, ed., *Ein Sprung in der Kette vom Zolibat*, Solingen, 1985 (Privately printed.) See also, Ursula Goldmann-Posch, *Unheilige Ehen: Cesprache mit Priesterfrauen*, Munich, Kindler Verlag, 1988.

23. Michael Miles, *Love is Always*, New York, Morrow, 1986, p. 326.

24. Beifuss, *op. cit.*, p. 19.

25. Carol Gilligan, *In a Different Voice*, Cambridge, Harvard University Press, 1982, p. 6.

Chapter Nine

Children of Resigned Priests

Most American Catholic priests who resigned the active ministry since Vatican II, got married and soon thereafter—not unexpectedly—began to father children. Many of these youngsters are now teenagers ready to talk about their experiences. In this country we face a brand new Catholic phenomenon: a unique generation of Catholic "preachers' kids" whose fathers no longer live in parish rectories or religious communities. Many stories have been told about Protestant ministers' children who are brighter, more religious and better behaved than the children of non-clergy parents. There is also the stereotype of the rebellious youth who is "fed up" with too much religion in the family and fails to do credit to his parents. If we are to accept Spence's classic autobiography as normative, the average preacher's kid is neither a paragon nor a prodigal.[1] There is, of course, the popular rumor that the children of ministers, more than those of other professionals, are listed in *Who's Who*.

The experience of priests' wives in the Episcopal Church suggests that they do not want their children "set apart" as models for other families. Only three out of ten (28%) say that they expect their children to behave better than other children, but most of them (79%) do not feel that the parishioners have such expectations of the parsonage children.[2] One Episcopal priest remarked, "When they're little they get too much attention. They start off living in a fish bowl, and you have to protect your children from that." We have little information, other than hearsay and fiction, about preachers' children in the larger Protestant churches.

The priests' children we tell about here do not live in a parsonage, but they ought to be a special kind of young Catholic because their parents belong to the National Association for a Married Priesthood, known previously as CORPUS (Corps of Reserve Priests United for Service). In the CORPUS *Directory* of 1990,[3] we found 217 clergy couples with 554 children, of whom 385 are "young adults" (fifteen years of age and older). We excluded children from a previous marriage of the mother, in order to avoid the special problem of step-children. The brief two-page questionnaire we sent to each of these youngsters drew 233 completed and usable responses, an appreciable return rate of 61 percent. Two-thirds of them are teenagers still in high school, and the answers came from more girls than boys (54% to 46%). They reside in all nine U. S. Census regions, with most in the Mid-West and fewest in the South. Three out of five (61%) of the fathers were diocesan priests, and more than half (55%) of the mothers had been religious Sisters.

What do these youngsters say about themselves and their parents? Are they just normal Catholic teenagers, or are they something more, and different? One high-school girl said, "being the child of a priest is no different than being the child of a doctor or a lawyer." One male respondent, however, a college sophomore, said that he can "sense" the persons who come from priest-families. "I can still pick out an ex-priest, or an ex-nun, just by their movement, action and vocabulary alone. Growing up with a priest-father is a very interesting experience, especially having Mass at home."

The father of this young man remarked, "What we have seen in our experience so far is that the children of resigned priests, especially if both the mother and the father were from religious life, are quite unusual, quite different. They're very well adjusted, but they certainly are different from the run-of-the-mill kids who are just looking to get the big job with the big buck. They seem to have a lot better values in life, or at least different values, from what their classmates have."

In setting the "stage" for the description of these children of Catholic priests, two cautions must be made: The first is that they are not strictly comparable to the children of Protestant ministers' families. They do not live in a parish rectory (less than one in ten would like to live in a parsonage, if their parents were returned to the active ministry). This means that they escape the kind of parishioner scrutiny that preachers' kids have to endure.[4] While seven out of ten say that their parents are active in "church work," they are talking about the kind of volunteer activity common to the Catholic laity. For the most part, their friends know that their father is a priest, but this causes little or no embarrassment for them.

The second caution is to note that the 233 respondents to this survey are not a representative sample of all married priests' families. They authentically reflect only the membership of the National Association for a Married Priesthood. We have no reliable knowledge of the thousands of other families of married resigned priests, who have not aligned themselves with the programs, plans and aspirations of CORPUS. Terrence Dosh estimates that there are at least 17,000 resigned married priests in the United States, of whom about 5,000 want to return to the active ministry. We may surmise that they differ appreciably from the families we are here studying. In other words, the families here under study are probably "closer" to the Church, and "more Catholic" than the great majority of other non-canonical priests' families.

We are therefore without a "control group" of clergy families, either Protestant or Catholic, with whom statistical comparisons can be made. As a partial substitute we are able to make comparisons with the responses of 244 Catholic college first-year students who answered some of the same questions on religious practices, moral values and social attitudes.[5] The two categories are roughly comparable in age, gender and educational experience.

Clergy Parents

The fathers in these families, and many of the mothers, took up a second sacramental vocation when they switched from the celibate to the married life. It was a "delayed" vocation, as well as a delayed parenthood, since they were on the average about ten years older than the age when most Americans marry. "One of the things you notice is that your father is older than other fathers." One girl complained that "the Church prevented him from marrying and having a family earlier." A high-school senior remarked: "If my Dad wasn't a priest, he would have had me sooner." Another high-school boy said, "My Dad is usually very serious and never has taken enough time to just have fun."

Except for a few (9%) who are retired, most of the fathers are in college and high-school teaching, in educational administration and counseling, or some form of social welfare activity. Only one-third (32%) are in the "business" world, as in management, advertising and sales. In reporting on the economic status of their family, hardly any (5%) of the respondents say that they are "poor," while one-third (35%) are "well off," with the remaining majority in the middle-income class.[6] Family income is augmented by mothers who are gainfully employed, mainly in teaching and nursing, but also in social work, secretarial and sales positions.

In this survey of young adults in clergy families we have no intention of passing moral judgments about their parents, but we are curious to know whether they share the CORPUS goal of readmission to the active ministry. Three out of ten (28%) think that their father has no intention, or expectation, of returning to the canonical priesthood. More than twice as many (63%) are sure that he wants to come back to the official priestly ministry. One out of five (19%) reports that the Vatican has not granted a dispensation from priestly vows, with permission to marry. The majority (73%), however, are aware that their father has gone through the process of "laicization." One gets the impression that this formal rescript—"just a piece of paper"—is not taken seriously by either parents or children.

It is traditionally "unusual," of course, that young Catholics can refer to their father as a priest (or, as a few insist, "he *was* a priest)." They see no reason for hiding the identity of their father, nor do they feel that there is any "stigma" attached to the fact of priestly paternity. Nine out of ten say their friends know the situation and either give approval or "couldn't care less." In a few instances they complained that there was "just too much religion" in the family. "We were constantly going to Mass and other church things. It was really too much." One young woman, whose mother had been a nun for twenty years, said, "I feel that religion was 'shoved down my throat,' causing me to have negative feelings about the Church."

One college girl, who also had an ex-nun mother, said that her parents had difficulty in relating to teenagers because they had spent their youth in the seminary and the convent, and had never experienced a "normal adolescence." On the other hand, a college co-ed wrote: "My father has set an example of humility, gentleness, compassion, deep love, and faith." A younger high-schooler said, "I like the rebellious attitude my Dad has toward the Church. It has given me a healthy perspective which he transferred to me. He is not anti-Church but says we have to be productively critical." In a lighter vein, a high-school senior said, "the parents of my dates trust me more." Furthermore, "to tell the story that your parents were a priest and a nun is a great ice-breaker at parties."

Ex-Nun Mothers

More than half (55%) of the young respondents to this survey are the children of former religious Sisters. This is a higher proportion of ex-nuns than we sampled (40%) from the Hegarty Directory.[7] The early study, sponsored by the American Bishops in 1972, found that 43 percent of the wives of resigned priests had been members of religious communities.[8] Maureen Hendricks employed a kind of "snowball" sampling to reach her married couples, of whom half the wives were ex-nuns.[9] Because the CORPUS membership, from which we reached our respondents, has a special apostolic ideology, we may surmise that it is attractive to former nuns.

There are no reliable statistics reporting the number of married resigned priests, much less the number of former women religious who married these priests. In the jargon of a simplistic psychology, one may suggest that there is a love-hate relationship between ex-nuns and the Catholic Church. If they had negative reasons for leaving the convent, they may remain critical of Catholicism. On the other hand, they are married to priests who want to get back into the active priesthood and bring their wives with them. This ambivalence toward Church and religion may help to explain some of the responses of their children.

Have their children demonstrated a level of spiritual behavior that may be attributed to their mother's influence? Are there differences between the children of ex-nun mothers and the other children? In answer to the question, whether religion "gives meaning" to their lives, the children of ex-nuns are less likely (61% to 75%) to answer affirmatively. This is about the same percentage difference (66% to 80%) in response to the question, whether they have a "personal relationship" with God. In the comparison of external religious practices, like attending Mass ("often" 65% to 77%) and receiving Holy Communion ("often" 65% to 72%), the children of ex-nuns are in lower proportions. For some unknown reason, the ex-nuns are less likely (46% to 60%) to send their children to Catholic schools. There is also less attraction to the church vocation among the children of ex-nuns (24% to 32%), and a greater distaste for the prospect of living in a parsonage with their parents (76% to 65%).

Would the religious Sister insist that her man have a Church dispensation before marrying her? We assumed that the children would know whether or not their father had been dispensed from priestly obligation and therefore eligible for valid sacramental marriage. Only a small minority (8%) said they did not know the answer. One out of five (19%) knows that the dispensation has not been received. The comparative statistics show that the ex-nun mothers are more than twice as likely (25% to 11%) to have married a non-dispensed priest, and are thus living in an "invalid" marriage. Another hypothesis is that the ex-nun mothers would eagerly promote their husband's return to the active ministry. This is not the case (as interpreted by their children). Approximately seven out of ten have husbands willing to return, but the ex-nuns show no greater enthusiasm than the other wives about returning to the canonical priesthood.

Six out of ten (61%) of the mothers are married to resigned diocesan priests, the remainder to men from religious orders. (This approximates the national statistics of 65% diocesan men in the active ministry). A higher proportion (69%) of ex-nuns, than of the other mothers (52%), have married diocesan priests. Couples in which the husband had been a religious order priest are less likely to engage in "church work" (21% to 41%) and their children are also less likely (46% to 56%) to be active parishioners. We can only speculate why there are such disproportions. The great majority of diocesan priests—as compared to religious-order priests—are engaged in ministry at the parish level; and it is likely that Sisters teaching in the parochial schools meet their future husbands in that setting.

Catholic Identity

All the children of resigned priests were baptized and confirmed in the Catholic Church and had received their first Holy Communion, but about half (48%) of them had not attended Catholic elementary or secondary school. Two-thirds of them are still in high school, and only a minority (16%) report attendance at both levels of Catholic education. We wanted to know whether they identify with the institutional Church through parish membership, which would ordinarily be the case with Catholic school students. Half of these children, however, admit that they are not active in their local parish, except for attendance at Sunday Mass (when they do go to church). The others do participate in a variety of ways: in CCD classes and study groups, as ushers, lectors, and choir members.

Most of the respondents are "practicing" Catholics, some of them enthusiastically so. They appear to be quite content to accept the religious counsel and guidance of their parents. It is the exception who has negative feelings about Catholicism, like the high-school girl who said, "I don't consider myself a Catholic. I feel that my ambivalence is due to the fact that my father left the priesthood. Right now, Quakerism looks to be the most appealing religion to me. I am at a stage in my life when I am questioning everything." Another youth said, "I'm not sure what I believe, but I am moving toward Buddhism."

The common criteria for the measure of active Catholicism are in the frequency of Mass and the sacraments.[10] We asked these youngsters about their attendance at Mass during the past two years, and the great majority (69%) said that they have "often" gone to Mass. They gave the same proportional response about the frequency of receiving Holy Communion. In about one-third (36%) of these families, Mass attendance is "made easy" for the children because their father regularly celebrates Mass at home or among the neighbors. No one raised a question about violation of the Vatican prohibition of celebrating the Eucharist by non-canonical priests.

When asked about the sacrament of Reconciliation, "going to confession," the great majority (73%) report that they "seldom" (31%) or "never" (42%) had entered the confessional during the past two years.[11] We did not ask them about their habits of personal prayer, but almost eight out of ten (78%) admit that they seldom, or never, read the Bible.

We asked no direct question about their own moral conduct to indicate the degree to which they conform to the ethical tenets of the Catholic religion. Interestingly enough, only one out of five (21%) "depends on the Church for moral guidance" (girls, 26%, more than boys, 14%). We asked them to make a judgment about several forms of moral behavior. The label of "always wrong" was placed proportionately on the following items: cheating on term papers or exams, 77%; telling racial and ethnic jokes, 43%, drunkenness, 33%, and pre-marital sexual relations, 21%.[12]

There are some gender differences of judgment about these moral actions that may be somewhat unexpected. They did not differ on the proportions who think that cheating is always wrong. We find, however, that a larger percentage of girls (87%) than of boys (75%) think that telling racial and ethnic jokes is "always" and "sometimes" wrong. On the other hand, a higher percentage of boys (79% to 68%) hold that pre-marital sex is "always" or "sometimes" wrong. On the matter of drinking too much, there is little gender difference of opinion (73% to 71%).

One may suggest in these gender comparisons that the values of the secular culture are held more firmly than the values of Church teachings. It is clear that the Church is more concerned than the secular society about the virtues of sobriety and chastity.[13] On the other hand, the general culture of the American society tends to find fault with cheating and with racial slurs.

One may hypothesize that the children of Catholic clergy parents are more Catholic in their beliefs and practices than children who were raised in otherwise "normal" Catholic families. We have used some of the same questionnaire items in a survey of 244 first-year students of a Catholic college. There are similarities, for example, in the proportions who have a personal relationship with God and who agree that religion gives meaning to life. An interesting difference is that the children of priests are less likely (21%) than the college students (34%) to say that they look to the Church for moral guidance. Nevertheless, the children of priests are much more likely than the college students to attend Mass and receive Communion "often."

Thinking with the Church

Despite the pressure for change, it is still the "thinking of the Church," as expressed in solemn Vatican documents, that priests of the Latin rite should not be married men. The very existence of a category of priests who have married and become fathers of a family is a reversal of the centuries-old tradition of a celibate priesthood. The young respondents of this survey are, of course, overwhelmingly in agreement that "diocesan priests be allowed to marry." It has been the continual aspiration and hope of their parents, as members of CORPUS, that the celibacy provision be removed from the Church's procedures and that they themselves be readmitted as married priests. Their children logically support the aims of CORPUS.

In another opinion that is also clearly in opposition to current thinking among the Church hierarchy, these youngsters voted (71%) in favor of the ordination of women to the priesthood.[14] In this instance, they appear to be more liberal than their parents, who had discussed this matter at great lengths in the several annual conferences of the National Association for a Married Priesthood. Clergy wives, the mothers of these young Catholics, had sometimes argued that a crusade for women's ordination might distract from their own primary goal of their husband's reinstatement in the institutional priesthood. It is an interesting fact that one-fifth of the young people did not express an opinion, either pro or con, on the matter of women's ordination, and only a few of them (8%) were in opposition. It is probably to be expected that the girls (77%) were more likely than the boys (64%) to favor the introduction of women clergy to the Catholic Church.

The "mind" of the Church is expressed also in the pastoral letters published by the American hierarchy, and we checked on whether these young people pay attention to them. It is quite clear that the American Bishops have great concern for the poor people of our nation and favor adequate welfare payments to the needy. Seven out of ten (73%) of our young respondents are also in favor of continued support of the public welfare program. This is, of course, the general attitude of liberal and progressive Catholicism, and reflects the social philosophy of the Holy Father as well as of the U. S. hierarchy.

There are two other social issues about which the bishops have made known their moral teaching: the abolition of the death penalty for convicted criminals, and the support of immigrant aliens. Slightly less than half (47%) of the respondents, but more girls (52%) than boys (41%) feel that the death penalty should be abolished. About half (52%) of these youngsters, but again, more girls (59%) than boys (43%) feel that illegal alien immigrants should not be deported from the United States. The tendency among conservative Catholics is to look upon these social issues as matters of politics, where the bishops are "out of their field," rather than as obligations of community morality.

Many of these youngsters did not have the benefits of formal Catholic education, in which the more debatable issues of public policy are part of the curriculum. Nevertheless, they are far out in front of the Catholic college students in their support of the bishops' social teaching. They are much stronger in favor of social welfare for the poor (73% to 43%); more in favor of help to alien immigrants (52% to 18%), and in opposition to the death penalty (47% to 26%). The parental influence for progressive social thinking has undoubtedly accounted for their children's attitude for social change. These youngsters have to be aware that their parents' decision to marry and found a family was in itself a demonstration of "progressive" social thinking.

Transitional Teens

Parents often remark the changing moods and attitudes of their teenage children, and our data allow us to make comparisons between the 76 youngest respondents, all of whom are in high school, and the 76 oldest, all collegians. We may hypothesize that with the passage of years they have a deeper understanding and a greater appreciation of growing up in the family of a resigned priest. Many studies have shown, however, that spiritual and religious values tend to lessen during the teen years, and moral values decline. Adolescents tend to move away from Church attendance and religious practices as they get into the college years. [15]

Being away at college probably helps to explain why the older respondents are almost twice as likely (65% to 34%) to report that they do not participate in their local parish. There is also a significant drop in the frequency of Mass attendance (79% to 53%), as well as in the reception of Holy Communion (82% to 49%). A concomitant statistic is in the increase of those who never go to confession (from 30% to 53%). From the perspective of the priest's family such declines in religiosity may be disappointing, but the decline is even more notable among youth who do not have the experience of a priest-father's family.

There is, however, an unchanging undercurrent of personal spirituality among these youngsters. There are still seven out of ten (72%) at all three levels who say that they have a personal relationship with God, and also the consistent proportion (65%) who acknowledge that religion gives meaning to their lives. On the other hand, their filial dependence on the Catholic Church shows a decline in the area of moral guidance. The shift in those who do not depend on the Church for moral guidance is from 32 percent among the youngest to 47 percent among the oldest. One of the older college men says he has "difficulties with the traditional, conservative Catholic Church. I feel that the problems I have with the backwardness of our Church stem from my father's past."

Their love and appreciation for their clergy parents continue through the years, and in some aspects even increase. The proportion who said they were "enthusiastic" about having a priest-father doubled, from 16 percent to 32 percent, and the great majority at all age levels declared themselves quite "comfortable" about having clergy parents. Their comments and compliments increase as they get into the college years. One coed admires her father as a person of varied experience. "He's really had two careers, and is twice as interesting to talk with as anybody else. He's had a great variety of experiences." They tend to show sympathy for the problems their parents endured. One college senior who intends to enter the convent feels regret in "knowing my father is not able to do that which he most wants to do and that which I feel he would be best at doing, i.e., being a *practicing* priest."

Growing up in the family of a priest-father appears to present no hindrances to the development of the normal adolescent personality. Only a few of them remark that they are in an "unusual" or "unique" kind of Catholic family. Many who wrote comments on the questionnaire made the point that their parents were just "normal" parents, and said, "I do not think of myself as the child of a priest." As they grew older there were more friends who shared their "secret" and gave approval to them. In general, however, it appears that the "novelty" of clergy parents and priest-fathers has now worn off, or the older children have simply become used to it.

Church Vocations

It is a commonplace of biographical lore that parents generally are pleased when their children follow in the same profession or occupation.[16] This was impossible, of course, for Catholic priests before the revisions of the Canon Law in 1982. Priestly paternity had been a diriment impediment for ordination to the priesthood. In some Hispanic peasant communities the child of a priest was said to have *sangre sagrada*, a title of considerable respect. It is of specific interest, therefore, that almost three out of ten (28%) of these children are "considering" a church vocation. A higher percentage of boys (34%) anticipate the seminary, than of girls (22%) who may opt for the Sisterhood.[17] One high-schooler said, "Some people think I am going to automatically be a priest."

In seeking an explanation for the relatively large interest in church vocations, we surmised the priest-father would have an influence in this direction. Indeed, they were much more ready (55% to 18%) to say that they are "enthusiastic" about having a priest-father. They report certain aspects of their fathers that indicate favorable attitudes to church vocation. In comparison with respondents who are not interested in religious vocation they, in larger proportion (69% to 59%), are willing to return to active ministry; have received the dispensation (80% to 71%), and actually celebrate Mass (45% to 32%).

The beliefs and behavior of these prospective church personnel differ significantly from the other respondents. They are more than twice as likely (83% to 37%) to report that they are involved in parish activities. They belong to the youth clubs, act as ushers and acolytes, are lectors and choir members. Four out of five (80%) attend Mass "often," and also (83%) receive Holy Communion. Like all respondents, they seldom go to confession, but they are much more likely (36% to 13%) to read the Bible regularly.

In the area of personal spirituality it appears that the prospective vocations are "closer to God." We asked if they have a personal relationship with God, and they answered affirmatively (92% to 65%). They said also that religion gives meaning to their lives (86% to 59%). In the several questions we asked about morality, the vocations were consistently more aware of wrong behavior; especially on pre-marital sex relations (36% to 14%)—they think it always wrong.

One wonders whether the mothers who previously had the experience of religious Sisterhood advise daughters to follow in their footsteps. We have seen above, that the children of ex-nuns are less likely (24%) than the children of other mothers (32%) to express interest in the church vocation. Neither do they demonstrate greater spirituality than the others in their spiritual practices and religious beliefs. Nor are they as likely to express an interest in religious life. These women resigned the religious vocation and married a resigned priest, but we do not know the measure of their dissatisfaction with their life in the convent. Obviously the vows of religion preclude the option of marriage for nuns. Certainly the contemporary life of women religious is vastly different from a generation ago.

Prospective seminarians, however, may vaguely hope for a change in the celibacy demands of the priesthood. They have become accustomed to family life, with a married priest as their father, and they are almost universally in favor of a married priesthood. In the current legislation of the Church they are aware that they cannot follow their father into marriage and family. Yet, the proportion of these priests' children who show interest in the church vocation is higher than any other category of youths outside the seminary. One may ironically suggest to vocation recruiters that the best source of vocations to the priesthood is among the sons of priests who are not allowed to function as priests.

Endnotes

1. Hartzell Spence, *Get Thee Behind Me*, New York, Whittlesey, 1942.

2. John and Linda Morgan, *Wives of Priests*, Notre Dame, Parish Life Institute, 1980, pp. 33f.

3. The *Directory*, published in Minneapolis, and edited by Terence Dosh, National Coordinator of the National Association for a Married Priesthood, contains 1,060 entries (some of whom are friends and supporters of the Association).

4. It was thought "surprising" that 45 percent of the Episcopal priests' families "actually live in a Rectory owned by the parish." Morgan, *op. cit.*, p. 32.

5. *Loyola Students and Their Values*, New Orleans, 1987 (privately distributed by the Campus Ministry of Loyola University of the South).

6. Some dioceses now pay a "pension" to resigned priests who have served at least twenty years in the active ministry. These monthly payments begin at age seventy.

7. Joseph H. Fichter, "Wives Speak Out about Life with Father," *National Catholic Reporter*, March 23, 1990, p. 24.

8. *The Catholic Priest in the United States*, Washington, U. S. Catholic Conference, 1972, p. 287.

9. Maureen Hendricks, *A Study of the Marriages and Marital Adjustment of Resigned Roman Catholic Priests and Their Wives*, Greeley, University of Northern Colorado, 1979, p. iv.

10. In the families of Episcopalian priests, 92 percent report that their children "attend weekly worship." Morgan, *op. cit.*, p. 49.

11. Only 14 percent of teenagers went to confession during the past month, as reported by George Gallup and Jim Castelli, *The American Catholic People*, Garden City, Doubleday, 1987, p. 32.

12. On all four items Catholic first-year college students have lower percentages voting "always wrong:" cheating, 68%; racial slurs, 23%; drunkenness, 28%; pre-marital sex, 16%.

13. The wives of Episcopal priests are much more likely (90%) to condemn extra-marital sex than pre-marital sex (49%). Morgan, *op. cit.*, p. 76.

14. The 1985 Gallup Poll of Catholic laity shows 63 percent in favor of married priests, and 47 percent in favor of women priests. See George Gallup and Jim Castelli, *op. cit.*, p. 56.

15. The "classic" in this regard is the work of Dean Hoge, *Commitment on Campus: Changes in Religion and Values Over Five Decades*, Philadelphia, Westminster, 1974.

16. Yet, among the wives of Episcopal priests, only 18 percent would encourage a son to be a priest; 10 percent would discourage him, and the remainder would do neither. See Morgan, *op. cit.*, p. 164.

17. In a random sample of Catholic college students, Hoge found eight percent of men and five percent of women who had "seriously considered" a religious vocation. Dean Hoge, *The Future of Catholic Leadership*, Kansas City, Sheed & Ward, 1987, p. 123.

Chapter Ten

Bishops Ought to Marry

In a survey of diocesan priests (non-pastors and non-monsignors) in 1966 we asked whether they thought bishops ought to marry or remain celibate. Four out of ten (39%) replied that only celibates should be raised to the episcopate. On the other hand, an equal proportion (38%) said the bishops ought to marry. When asked about the pastorate the priests were much more ready (62%) to say that pastors should be married men.[1] Several surveys, made later by the National Federation of Priests' Councils, also discovered that more than six out of ten parish curates felt that diocesan priests should have the option to marry. Hardly anybody else discussed the prospect of married bishops, which at that time had to be an outlandish idea.

Optional Celibacy

Some accounts by observers at the Second Vatican Council gave the impression that the delegates were afraid to discuss the topic of a married clergy in the Western Church. As a matter of fact, when the debate began on the restoration of the diaconate, Cardinal Bacci of the Curia said it was "dangerous" because it would lead to the proposal that deacons be allowed to marry. Holy Orders and matrimony were to be kept in complete separation. It appears that no bishop had the temerity to suggest any change in the existing celibacy legislation on the floor of the Council debates. Everything else could be discussed, and one gets the impression that clergy marriage was a "fearful topic" but episcopal attitudes soon changed. In the Synod of 1971, Bishop Valfredo Tepe presented the majority opinion of the Brazilian hierarchy in favor of ordaining married men.[2]

The several American ex-bishops, who have since resigned and married, are probably a source of reflection and conversation among the hierarchy. They know that resignation from the episcopacy makes you an ex-bishop, but resignation from the active ministry cannot make you an ex-priest. The notion that a man has to stop being a bishop if he has a wife would have seemed strange to married deacons, priests and bishops in the early Church. For example, Synesius of Cyrene, said that he would consent to be Bishop of Ptolemais only if he would be "allowed to continue to have intercourse with his wife."[3] Such historical incidents tend to be downplayed, and the average lay person—and probably priest too—may be shocked by the thought of a married bishop. Even the Eastern Uniate Churches, where married men are routinely ordained, draw the line at married bishops.

The bishops of the Latin rite, including the Pope, make it collectively clear that they have no intention of changing the Canon Law that forbids priestly marriage.[4] Relatively few exceptions have been allowed for the ordination of married clergymen of other denominations. One of these exceptions was a married bishop of the Episcopal Church, Peter Watterson, who is now quietly ministering to the Catholic faithful in Florida. Otherwise, however, one may surmise that most of the American hierarchy are not attracted to the marriage vocation for themselves. They are past the normal marriageable age; they have patterned their lives as bachelors, and their status in the ecclesiastical structure persuades them to uphold the sacred value of clerical and episcopal celibacy. Moreover, they would probably find it functionally awkward to administer the diocese, if their priests were married and they remained celibate.

Generalizations of this kind, about "what the bishops think," must be made with great caution. We do not know how the Ordinaries of 188 dioceses and archdioceses would respond individually to an anonymous questionnaire. It appears to be a very sensitive question that Catholic sociologists hesitate to research. Jesuit Father Terrence Sweeney, who has since resigned the priesthood, found that 24 percent of his episcopal respondents favor optional clergy celibacy.[5] He was severely reprimanded by the Roman authorities for including the question of optional clergy celibacy (and of women's ordination) in a survey of the American hierarchy. This breach of clerical decorum was deemed so reprehensible that an attempt was made to suppress the anonymous statistics. In other words, episcopal opinions on this matter should remain secret.

One thing is certain about our bishops: Not all of them are traditionalists or conservatives. On occasion they have collectively and individually made progressive statements on important social issues: the faulty economic system, the dangers of nuclear weapons, the need for social welfare, and even women's liberation. There is about a thirty-year age span between the youngest and the oldest prelates. If attitudes toward marriage change as one grows older, it is quite probable that some of the younger prelates are in favor of optional celibacy for diocesan priests, and possibly even for bishops.

In a less than serious moment, I once proposed that when the reform comes in Church law on clerical celibacy there should be optional marriage for the priests, but mandatory marriage for the bishops.[6] Let us say that the mandate be only temporary, perhaps only for the next quarter-century, during the transitional period, or until the ecclesiastical structure has accommodated itself to this change. Bishops who now feel that they are too old to take a spouse will probably go to their heavenly reward during the next twenty-five years. Marriage as a qualifying condition for elevation to the episcopacy should be applied only to new candidates for the office. Thus, we may hopefully anticipate the selection of younger men for the hierarchy. If one change leads to another we may even expect a limited term of office for bishops. Bishop Paul Anderson, who resigned from Duluth in 1982, declared that the Ordinary of any diocese ought to retire after serving for one decade.

Back at the Council

In the prayerful deliberations of the Second Vatican Council there were no discussions about how to handle married priests, but the assembled prelates decreed that a bishop should have "special love" for his priests. "He should regard his priests as sons and friends." (*Christus Dominus*, art. 16) In another document they pointed out that bishops and priests share in the same ministry and priesthood, which means that "the bishop should regard priests as his brothers and friends." This is why he "should gladly listen to them, indeed, consult them." (*Presbyterorum Ordinis*, art. 7) This advice suggested a level of informal personal relationship with the priests, that downplayed previous notions of episcopal authority and prestige. Collegiality was not to be limited to relations with fellow bishops, but to be extended to the lower clergy who share in the priesthood of the hierarchy. The pastoral work of the entire diocese is promoted by his "readiness to listen to them and by his trusting familiarity."

When the American bishops returned from the Council, and while they were planning the implementation of their conciliar decisions, their diocesan priests were appraising bishop-priest relationships. We have seen, above, that they speculated about married bishops, but they also said that the most pertinent problem was the "lack of accessibility to the bishop by his priests." More than half of these lower-echelon clergy express a "negative opinion on the three important tests of bishop-clergy relations: the personal interest of the bishop, his communication with them, and the free and open communication in the diocesan structure as a whole."[7]

It was also at this very time that the bishops all over the country had to handle increasing requests for clergy dispensations. The bishops had hardly settled down to their ordinary diocesan tasks after the Council, when they were faced with a petition from the National Symposium on Clerical Celibacy, to "support the proposal that diocesan priests be permitted the option of marrying, or remaining celibate, while exercising the active ministry of the Church."[8] This symposium request coincided with the organization of the National Association for Pastoral Renewal in 1967, and with the research finding that 62 percent of the clergy respondents favored optional celibacy for priests, and that 92 percent agreed that married priests and their wives should be allowed to return to the sacraments."[9]

The onrush of requests for dispensations and the volume of resignations seemed to catch the bishops by surprise. While some bishops responded with pastoral solicitude to the requests of these priests, most of them seemed to be confused and at a loss what to do. "No priest in this situation goes to his bishop, except in fear and trembling, fully expecting to find no understanding, and this no matter how open and kind the bishop has shown himself to be in the past."[10] Robert Francoeur described some of the rebuffs suffered by priests. Some bishops denied them a hearing; some asked the priest to leave his parish immediately, even demanded that he move out of the diocese. In the end, the rescript has to come from Rome, and "it is practically impossible to get a clear idea what Rome considers 'sufficient reason' for granting an *ante factum* permission to marry."

Moment of Truth

Meanwhile, the National Federation of Priests' Councils had been organized in response to the needs of the lower clergy and in accord with the recommendations of the Second Vatican Council (*Christus Dominus*, art. 2). They instituted a clergy survey in 1969, directed by John Koval, and independent of the NCCB priest study. Their data "revealed that priests were dissatisfied with the leadership of those in authority, with the slow pace of change since Vatican II, with the failure of the Church to take a strong stand on social and moral issues, and with the laws of the Church forbidding priests to marry."[11] At the 1971 NFPC convention in Baltimore, the delegates voted nine-to-one in favor of changing the Church's law on celibacy. In their so-called "Moment of Truth" statement, they asked that "the choice between celibacy and marriage for priests now active in the ministry be allowed, and we call for the change to begin immediately."

This forthright resolution was met with either silence or a negative reaction by most of the American bishops. Nevertheless, the Federation itself, as a kind of collective voice for the country's priests, was highly valued by prelates like Cardinal John Deardon and Archbishop Philip Hannan. Out of this Federation grew the NCCB's New Committee on Priestly Life and Ministry, which appeared to many to be "an answer to the numerous NFPC attempts to establish a Department of Ministry in the Roman Catholic Church in this country."

In the great majority of American dioceses, relations between bishops and priests have become more cooperative than adversarial. Nevertheless, the current group of American Bishops probably still feel that they cannot openly express their liberal progressive attitudes. Even when they are in favor of a married clergy they have to be cautious about saying so. The Vatican continues to be vindictive about the priest "deserters," and is extremely reluctant to grant release from the vow of celibacy. In 1980 Justin Cardinal Durwajuowomo of Jakarta personally told John Paul II that he would resign, if the Pope refused to allow him to ordain married men. The Pope immediately accepted his resignation.[12]

The most spectacular example of conflict between the clergy and the hierarchy arose in the aftermath of the papal document, *Humanae Vitae* in 1968, when Patrick Cardinal O'Boyle penalized and suspended priests who criticized Pope Paul's teaching. He was called the "harshest of the papal defenders." The conflict revolved around three intertwined issues: birth control, freedom of conscience and authority. "In the case of Cardinal O'Boyle, these authority factors converged. He acted as the completely traditional leader in portraying monarchical leadership and a governance mentality; in using negative and exclusionary sanctions; in minimizing the professional autonomy of clergy, and in neglecting lay expertise in the birth-control issue."[13]

From the perspective of the individual diocesan priest, the continual complaint was the lack of "due process" in his relations with episcopal authority. If his obedience was to be "absolute," as some bishops seem to imply, there was no need to present the "other side." This harshness has since been largely allayed, but the years of the O'Boyle dispute were a period of increasing resignations. The survey of priests, instituted by the U. S. Catholic Conference, estimated that 3,413 priests resigned in the four years, 1966 to 1969. This survey revealed the attitudes of clergy who remained, as well as of clergy who resigned.

Both categories of priests were unhappy about the lack of satisfactory communication with diocesan and church authorities. What sort of changes did the resigned priests want to see in the Church? "The most frequently mentioned change was some sort of reform of the ecclesiastical governmental structure. A change in the law of celibacy was mentioned only one-third as often as governmental change when the respondents were asked to choose only one reform."[14] More and more priests were asking for dispensation from the active ministry. Some of the resignees voiced harsh complaints about their bishops: "We see you simply as figureheads, administrators. You should be alive, concerned with all the issues, not just abortion and Catholic education. You, above all, should be crusading for human rights. You are too remote, selfish and lazy."[15]

The U. S. Bishops also commissioned a psychological survey of American priests, which was reported by Eugene Kennedy and Victor Heckler in 1972, as well as *Historical Investigations*, by John Tracy Ellis. A further investigation of the theological study of the priesthood was done by Carl Armbruster, who presented a summary of his study before the Bishops' spring meeting in 1971. This report was rejected, and never published, allegedly because Armbruster could find no theological, or scriptural, basis for the refusal to ordain women and married men. The bishops, in conformity with the well-published prohibitions of the Vatican, could not do otherwise.

No one could mistake the attitude of Pope Paul VI, whose Holy Thursday homily in 1971 recalled the "betrayal of Judas," in association with the resignation of so many brother priests. "How can we fail to weep at the deliberate defection of some?

How can we not deplore the moral mediocrity that would find it natural and logical to break one's own promise" that had been solemnly professed before Christ and the Church?[16] If the Holy Father entertained a spirit of fraternal reconciliation, it was not demonstrated in comparing the resigned priest to Judas Iscariot.

Improved Relations

For purposes of comparison it is instructive to review the lowly status of diocesan curates in the period of Second Vatican. The overwhelming majority (93%) of respondents said there was no personnel committee in their diocese; they also reported (89%) the absence of a grievance committee. Seven out of ten (72%) said their diocese did not have a clergy senate. Nine out of ten felt there should be a definite retirement age for pastors, as well as bishops. Almost two-thirds (64%) said that priests should be allowed voluntary resignation, or honorable discharge, from the clergy.[17]

The experiences of a quarter-century, the election of better-educated bishops, and the steady decline in numbers of priests, have combined to change the bishops' ways of relating to priests. It is probably as true now as it was twenty-five years ago, that "dealing with church personnel issues is considered by church administrators as the most difficult job in an archdiocese." On the other hand, remarks Archbishop Kelly of Louisville, "the priests' Personnel Board is the greatest invention of Vatican II."[18]

The alleged autocratic behavior of some American preconciliar prelates is said to have been replaced by men who heeded the kindlier attitudes advised by the decree, *Christus Dominus*. In 1972 the Vatican published a set of "Norms" that described the qualities desirable in members of the hierarchy. They are obviously expected to be men of high moral integrity, "outstanding for their piety." The prospective candidates should be judged also for their "intellectual qualities, studies completed, social sense, spirit of dialogue and cooperation, openness to the signs of the times, praiseworthy impartiality, family background, health, age, and inherited characteristics."[19] It is said that the Apostolic Delegate, Jean Jadot, was influential during his period (1973-1980) in recommending progressive bishops.[20]

Whether or not the contemporary American Bishops are of a higher "quality" than their predecessors, they have a quite different status relationship with the men who resigned the active ministry. The priests who left in the early period after the Council are now at about the same age level as today's hierarchy. Many of them had been close friends, seminary classmates, fellow workers in the diocese. The bishops are no longer the older and more remote prelates, looking askance at the younger priests who wished to get married. In fact, American Bishops who still reluctantly accept the resignation of their priests sometimes experience the same loss in their own family. They have faced the departure of a priestly brother, a cousin, a nephew, who decides to follow the marital vocation. While this experience may not weaken their own clerical vocation, it tends to put clergy marriage in a more familiar perspective.

Evidence of cordial relations between bishops and resigned priests was provided at the Third Annual Conference of Married Priests, held at San Jose State University, in June, 1990. Many bishop members of the NCCB were meeting on the same weekend, on the campus of Santa Clara University, only a short distance from San Jose. CORPUS, as usual, invited the bishops to attend the conference, but none did. A small committee, however, headed by Bishop Donald Wuerl, invited CORPUS representatives for a discussion on the following day. This was a closed meeting, lasting more than an hour, at which the bishops were both "cordial and attentive."

The officers of CORPUS, led by President Anthony Padavano, brought their agenda to this discussion. They wanted closer relations with NCCB, by regular liaison with the Committee on Priestly Life and Ministry. They asked also for an opportunity to present their "case" to a full meeting of the NCCB. Padavano stressed the problem of priestless parishes and Massless Sundays. "It is doubtful," he said, "that priestly celibacy could hold out for another decade," and he predicted that "soon the majority of priests would not be observing celibacy." At a later prayer and singing session some of the bishops mingled with the friends, contemporaries and former classmates among the resigned clergy.

Replacing Adversarial Relations

The California confrontation between bishops and priests became confused on the same Saturday afternoon, when a group from the Berkeley School of Theology confronted the bishops with demands for women's ordination. They called themselves "Women in Ministry," and felt that their demonstration of song and prayer had been interrupted by the presence of married priests and their wives. Nevertheless, the bishops accepted them with friendly greetings, and a half-dozen bishops spoke informally with these women. This demonstration was much more peaceful and orderly than the typical feminist confrontations held so frequently in urban cathedrals on the occasion of priestly ordinations.

The presence of these non-CORPUS representatives of the Women's Conference was in contrast to a gradual pro-feminist atmosphere among the wives of resigned priests. It is only recently that the voices of these women began to speak on their own behalf. Under the prevalent CORPUS philosophy the attention of the women had been focused on their husbands, with the insistence on the right to full acceptance in the sacramental ministry. Reacceptance into the clerical ministry was their foremost goal. They were the wives of priests, and they sought no recognition for themselves except as legitimate spouses. They complained about the injustice that had been done to their husbands by the bishops who dismissed them and excluded them.

Now the pro-feminist voices began to be heard. At both the Second and the Third Annual CORPUS Conventions, the program included discussion panels of a pro-feminist nature. It was not only a question of wives' support for their husbands' restoration to the active ministry, but the place of women in the Church. Relatively few of the wives felt that they had a priestly vocation, but they were beginning to speak as pro-feminists favoring women's rights in general. Even the strongest feminists, however, feel that the crusade for women's ordination may slow down the restoration of married priests. "We are facing two issues: married clergy and women's ordination. If you insist on married clergy, you are promoting paternalism and clericalism. If you insist on women's ordination, you are promoting clericalism and elitism."

While the wives are deeply loyal to their priest husbands, they feel that the male leadership of CORPUS is only beginning to open to the broader influence of feminism. "I think CORPUS has had a large share of paternalism and clericalism. There are enough chauvinists among them to be reluctant to listen to the women's needs for equality." Another argued that God's calling has to embrace both husband and wife. The call of God to ministry is not only to the married priest, or the woman priest, but also to the combined vocation of priest-husband and wife.

The CORPUS complaint about the "double standard," which allows acceptance of married clergymen from other denominations, was usually kept at a low key. On several occasions the media publicized the collective protests of married priests, when they appeared at the ordination ceremony of one of the married convert priests. This was not considered good strategy by the CORPUS leadership who were anxious to befriend the bishops, or at least avoid irritating them. The wives of the resigned priests did not appear at these public protests. Meanwhile, the bishops are at pains to argue that there is no "double standard" involved, between the married convert priests seeking the true faith and the married resigned priests who have left their active ministry.

Bishops and Women

It is a classical axiom of American Catholic folklore that bishops are the most confirmed male chauvinists. The evidence is everywhere: starting with the prohibition against altar girls and ending with the refusal to ordain women deacons. These changes have been vigorously refuted in recent pastoral letters that condemned sexism within the Church and said that the inability to treat women with equality made questionable a man's vocation to the priesthood. Women should be available for employment at all administrative levels of the Church. They went so far as to "recommend that women participate in all liturgical ministries that do not require ordination."[21]

The bishops' Pastoral clearly repudiates male chauvinism and promotes Christian feminism within the Church. "This pastoral letter supports the efforts of feminists in general to liberate women from attitudes that stand in the way of women using their gifts and talents for the good of society and the Church. We want to respond to the challenge that feminist thinkers, writers, teachers, and speakers pose for persisting in our intent to eradicate the personal and structural forms of sexism documented in this pastoral."[22]

At the level of personal relations between bishops and women it is the American historical experience that bishops have always had to deal with women religious and their Provincials, women who held important positions in hospitals, schools and social-welfare ministries. The shortage of vocations and the resignation of so many Sisters tend to raise the episcopal esteem for these women. In some dioceses, Sisters have been appointed chancellor as well as tribunal advocates. An increasing number of women are found on diocesan pastoral councils and in parochial positions as pastoral administrators, assistants and associates.

In our survey of the wives of convert Episcopal priests, we found that nine out of ten report amicable relations with the Ordinary. There are a few instances in which the affectionate and familial term, "Pani," is used in reference to the priest's wife. Most of the wives of permanent deacons say that their local bishop takes a personal interest in them, encourages them warmly, especially during their husband's course of formation. Several bishops, convinced that women should be ordained permanent deacons, have cancelled the diaconate training program because Rome refuses to admit women to be permanent deacons.

The wives of resigned priests, especially those associated with CORPUS, tend to treat their bishops as adversaries. Some still complain bitterly at the unjust and "un-Christian" manner in which the bishop dismissed their husbands. This is the minority who object that the bishop "wishes we will go away," and forbids her husband any level of ministry. On the other hand, more than half (57%) are willing to say that their bishop is "very" or "somewhat" friendly to their husbands. In some dioceses the bishop invites married priest-couples for discussions and spiritual consultations. "He wanted to be friendly with us, and actually met with seven couples for a social evening." One auxiliary bishop who is a close friend of some of our men, "met frequently on an informal basis and predicted whether the next baby would be a girl or a boy."

Married Bishops

When a man becomes a bishop he does not break ties with friends and family. His primary attention is directed to many other persons and functions, but he is not completely distracted from familial relations. Despite the rigid distinction drawn between celibate and married clergy in the modern Latin Church, there must still be far-distant recollections when not only priests, but also bishops and popes were married men. One thinks nostalgically of those early Christian communities where there were close relations between the clergy and the laity, and where the bishop mingled freely and intimately with all his flock.

My reasons for suggesting a return to the married hierarchy are sociological rather than theological or scriptural. Historically, the so-called Apostolic Age provides existential support for this proposal. The contemporary renewed appreciation of the early Christian community should include acceptance of the fact that most of the early popes, bishops, priests, and deacons were married men. Everyone knows Paul's admonition to Timothy, that the bishop has to be able to manage his family well, bring up his children in obedience. "How can any man who does not understand how to manage his own family have responsibility for the Church of God?" (I Tim. 3:5)

The quest for community in the modern out-size parish and large-scale diocese is thwarted by the social distance between the people and their bishop. Social stratification has been institutionalized to the point where the Church has multiple layers of status, from the lowliest lay person to the highest prelate, with all kinds of official and unofficial functionaries in between. It is rational that large-scale organizations are structured and stratified, even when modern techniques are employed to improve internal communications. In spite of the counter-weight of traditional customs, efforts are being made to reduce the negative effects of bigness and bureaucracy.

Requests for change in the law of celibacy have been centered on the diocesan clergy at the lower level. We should be aware, however, that if the priests marry and the bishops stay single, a new wedge of separation will be introduced into the Christian community. This is a sociological expectation, based on the historical experience of the Eastern rite churches, where the married priest stays at the lowest rung of the ecclesiastical ladder. He had no hope of promotion in his priestly career, because all of the important higher positions in the Church were reserved for celibates. He is often assigned to the least desirable parishes, in the most poverty-stricken areas, and was treated as a second-class citizen by his celibate fellow priests.

It may be argued that this would not happen in the United States, that the American cultural system is very different from that of the countries where the Eastern rite churches exist; and that an openly mobile society like ours would not succumb to the rigid stratification of the East. On the other hand, the lower-echelon diocesan clergy of the United States are already at the bottom of the ecclesiastical structure, and would probably remain there even if married. The career structure is quite flat, allowing only one promotion to the pastorate. Marriage may be a mobile advantage, if eventually the pattern of Protestant denominations is followed; that is, only married men are acceptable for the pastorate.

Since the Second Vatican Council, many changes have been introduced to accommodate the status and role of the diocesan priest; yet, the clamor for a married priesthood continues to be heard. What contribution could this make to pastoral renewal, to improved ministry in the Christian community, and especially—in the present context—to a reformation of human relations within the ecclesiastical structure? As one perceptive curate remarked, "even in the present situation the bishop is unable to understand his priests, and this situation would become impossible, if some of his clergy were married and he were not."

When the Church law on clerical celibacy is abrogated the question becomes one of tactics: How, and at what level, would married priests be introduced into the system? Alert priests see the answer in the "pastoral provisions" introduced for married convert priests. As a temporary and experimental procedure, married clergy should be assigned to specialized work, like teaching, direction of diocesan bureaus, chancery functions, and chaplaincies of various kinds. From a structural perspective, these are intermediary between the people and the prelates. Other married priests could sustain themselves and their families with full-time secular occupations, while helping out in "priestless" parishes and in large urban parishes that are now increasingly short-handed.

The Children

Marriage has consequences in the form of progeny. Unless there were some cautionary qualifications, that bishops and priests were allowed to marry only women beyond the child-bearing age—or women who are biologically sterile—another problem of social stratification may arise. One of the important historical side-effects of clerical celibacy in the Latin rite has been the absence of an hereditary "priestly caste." Even the earlier practice of nepotism has largely, if not entirely, disappeared. Yet, upward mobility has been possible in the Church where the son of an illiterate peasant can become a pontiff.

Sons of Protestant ministers and of Jewish rabbis are often attracted to the occupation of their father. It is said that the first women who petitioned for ordination in the Episcopal Church were daughters of the clergy. It is thinkable that the sons of Catholic priests and bishops would also want to enter the seminary—and could thus help alleviate the clergy shortage. The hypothetical question then arises, whether the sons of bishops would enjoy ecclesiastical preferment over the sons of priests, and thus introduce a career problem that does not currently exist in the Catholic Church. One may argue an antidote to this eventuality. Married priests and bishops—and their families—would help narrow the status gap presently existing between clergy and laity, and promote closer community relations within the Church.

Furthermore, if functional distance from the parishioners is the pragmatic criterion, why not go all the way and say that prelates and bishops, including the Pope, should be the first to marry, to marry young women, and have large families? Here, of course, we encounter another sociological problem: the population explosion. Up to now, the Catholic Church in America has made a genuine contribution to population control by withdrawing a quarter-million functionaries from biological reproduction. No other major religious denomination can make that boast. On the other hand, as the late Professor Dorothy Dohen once remarked, "the moral problems of contraception and planned parenthood might be solved more quickly if the Catholic clergy were married. Social change has latent as well as manifest functions."

As everyone must be aware, the proposal that prelates be the first to marry reverses the structure and procedures of the Eastern rite churches, where the upper-status clergy are celibates and the lower clergy has the option to marry before ordination. The American Bishops have occasionally discussed continuity and change in the Church. Bishops have no desire to "discourage the positive forces developing in the American Catholic Church." Rationality and calculation are characteristic of Western civilization, particularly of Anglo-Saxon culture, in the planning and development of social organizations. Changes and improvement are more readily acceptable here than elsewhere in the world.

In this kind of society, one would hope that the celibacy debate will be settled on the basis of pragmatic rationality rather than on a basis of tradition and preconception. Strict upholders of Church legislation claim that the debate is over, and the Pope excludes the topic from the Synod of Bishops. This is in keeping with the revised Code of Canon Law of 1983, stating flatly that "clerics are obliged to observe perfect and perpetual continence" and are, therefore, "obliged to observe celibacy, which is a special gift of God." (Can. 277.n. 1) With all reverence due to the Church lawgiver, one may still suggest that there are arguments against universal clerical celibacy. When the change is put into effect it seems reasonable to include bishops and other Church dignitaries in the option.

Endnotes

1. Joseph H. Fichter, *America's Forgotten Priests*, New York, Harper and Row, 1968, chapter 8, "Married Clergy."

2. Bonaventure Kloppenburg, *The Priests*, Chicago, Franciscan Herald, 1974, "Ordaining Married Men," p. 134.

3. *The Letters of Synesius of Cyrene*, quoted by Peter Brown, *The Body and Society*, New York, Columbia University Press, 1988, p. 292.

4. See, however, Pat Windsor, "Weakland willing to propose married priests," *National Catholic Reporter*, January 18, 1991, p. 3.

5. Terrence Sweeney, "Attitudes of U. S. Catholic Bishops on Priestly Ministers," 1986 (Unpublished Report). Bishops under age 50 were four times more likely than bishops over 70, to approve optional celibacy for priests.

6. Joseph Fichter, "Bishops Ought to Marry," *Commonweal,* 1968, vol. 88, pp. 289-291.

7. Fichter, *America's Forgotten Priests,* chap. 3, "The Priest-Bishop Relationship."

8. George Frein, ed., *Celibacy: The Necessary Option,* New York, Herder and Herder, 1968, p. 15.

9. Fichter, *op. cit.,* p. 177.

10. Robert Francoeur, *"Clerical Marriages: Ante and Post Factum,"* in Frein, *op. cit.,* 161-174.

11. See the account by Francis F. Brown, *Priests in Council,* Kansas City, Andrews and McMeel, 1979, p. 23.

12. Editorial, "Indonesia Challenges Rome," *CORPUS Reports,* September/October, 1990.

13. John Seidler and Katherine Meyer, *Conflict and Change in the Catholic Church,* New Brunswick, Rutgers University Press, 1989, p. 96.

14. Bishops' Survey: *The Catholic Priest in the United States,* Washington, U. S. Catholic Conference, 1972, p. 308.

15. *Ibid.,* p. 305.

16. Pope Paul VI, "Reflections on the Last Supper," (April 8, 1971) *The Pope Speaks,* vol. 16-17, pp. 8-12.

17. Fichter, *America's Forgotten Priests,* 62-66.

18. Thomas J. Reese, *Archbishop: Inside the Power Structure of the American Catholic Church,* San Francisco, Harper & Row, 1989, pp. 194 and 211.

19. "Norms for the Selection of Candidates for the Episcopacy in the Latin Church," *Origins,* May 25, 1972, pp. 1-9.

20. Reese, *op. cit.,* pp. 41f.

21. The first draft of the bishops' pastoral response was "Partners in the Mystery of Redemption," *Origins,* April 21, 1988. The second is "One in Christ Jesus," *Origins,* April 5, 1990. Distribution of the final draft has been delayed.

22. "One in Christ Jesus," par. 131.

Index